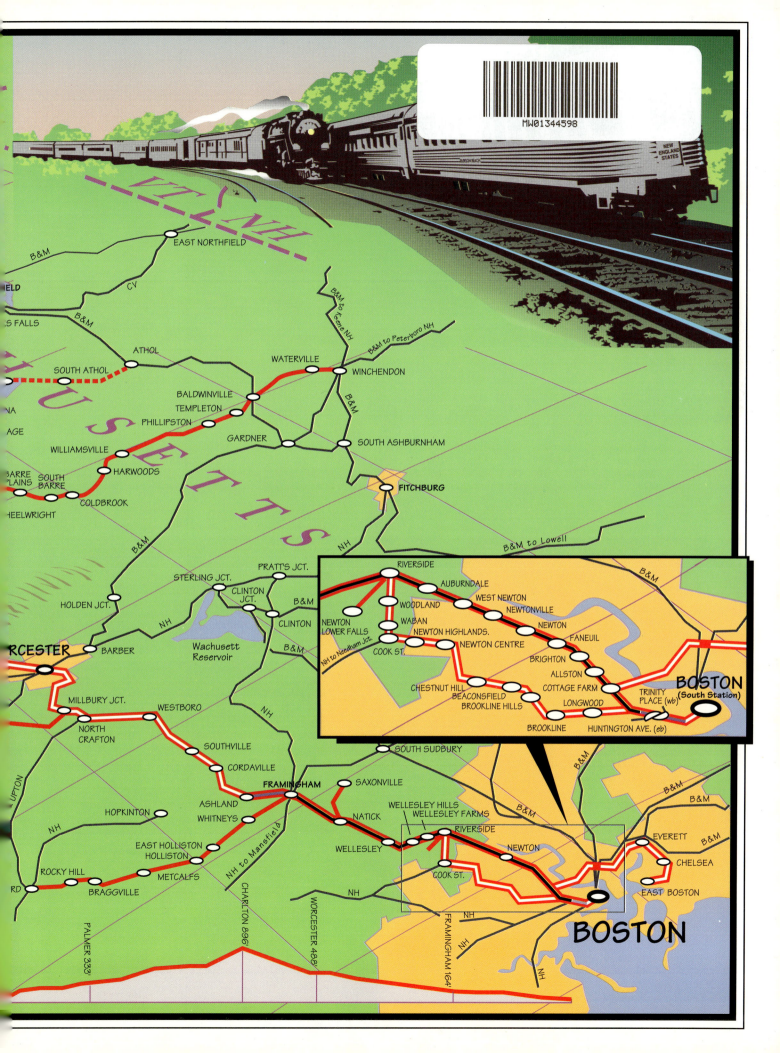

BOSTON & ALBANY

The New York Central in New England

Volume I: Boston to Worcester

THE NEW YORK CENTRAL IN NEW ENGLAND

VOLUME I: BOSTON TO WORCESTER

by Robert Willoughby Jones

Pine Tree Press - Los Angeles, California

FRONT COVER: A New York Central freight is southbound from Chatham, New York, on the Harlem Division on Thursday, February 15, 1951. Boston & Albany No. 586, a K-14g class 4-6-2 Pacific, is blasting up the grade in Philmont, New York. Stephen R. Payne photo.

REAR COVER ABOVE: Winter lingers past its welcome this April 1960 day as a lone NYC Budd RDC is outbound on Track 3 through the falling snow near Trinity Place station. Buried in the snow are four B&A and four NH tracks. At Back Bay station, just ahead, the New Haven's tracks will turn southwest for Providence, New Haven, and New York City. The Knickerbocker Beer billboard sits above the "town" end of NH Back Bay station. The layout here will change dramatically in a few years with the coming of the Massachusetts Turnpike Extension. In the distance a Main Line Elevated train is crossing high overhead (after 1966 it would be called the Orange Line). Fred Matthews photo.

REAR COVER BELOW: On an early 1950s day rich with saturated green and blue, the westbound *Knickerbocker* has just passed through Turtle Bend, just west of Russell. On the point is NYC RS-3 No. 8314 with a sister unit, two express cars, and six passenger cars. Thomas J. McNamara photo.

FRONTISPIECE: NYC E-8 No. 4094 passes the stationary E-8 No. 4047 at Framingham on Thursday, April 18, 1968. These are likely both commuter trains, the one at left with its steam activated, poised with a local train to Boston.

OPPOSITE TABLE OF CONTENTS: No. 1445 is on her hands and knees with a westbound freight at Rochdale in October 1948. This classic Berkshire locomotive was a 2-8-4, Class A-1c, built by Lima Locomotive Works in 1930. Stanley H. Smith photo/Norton D. Clark collection.

FRONT END PAPER: A system map of the Boston & Albany as it existed circa 1947. Most connecting railroads are shown, although the map is not to scale. The artist is John Signor.

REAR END PAPER: Through the generosity of Malcolm Woronoff of Aerial Photos, International, Inc. of Boston, we are able to provide this aerial view of South Station taken June 22, 1936, providing splendid detail of the terminal facility. The U. S. Post Office building which straddles several of the high-numbered tracks is very new. At the lower left is the former Boston & Albany Kneeland Street station, here relegated to use as a freight facility. Readers will note that the photo was made just a few minutes prior to the companion North Station view in BOSTON & MAINE—*Three Colorful Decades of New England Railroading*.

The quotation on page 39 is reprinted with the permission of Scribner, an imprint of Simon & Schuster from OF TIME AND THE RIVER by Thomas Wolfe. Copyright 1935 Charles Scribner's Sons; copyright renewed © 1963 Paul Gitlin, Administrator C. T. A.

The quotations on pages 18 and 98 are reprinted from LOST BOSTON by Jane Holtz Kay, copyright 1980 by Houghton Mifflin Co. Reprinted by permission of the author.

BOSTON & ALBANY—THE NEW YORK CENTRAL IN NEW ENGLAND—VOLUME I

© 1997 by Robert Willoughby Jones. All rights reserved.

No part of this book may be used or reproduced without written permission
from the publisher, except in the case of brief quotations used in reviews.

Layout and design by the author
Cover design by Katie Danneman
Chapter head illustrations by Pamela Jones Aamodt
Color separations by Complete Color, Glendale, California
Printing and Binding by Walsworth Publishing Company, Marceline, Missouri
Manufactured in the United States of America
First Printing: Summer 1997

ISBN 0-9640356-1-8
Published by Pine Tree Press
P. O. Box 39484, Los Angeles, California 90039

In memory of Leon Onofri

devoted husband and father who loved New England railroads
and whose photography has figured so prominently in my books

TABLE OF CONTENTS

Volume I: Boston to Worcester

Foreword 8

Acknowledgements 14

Introduction 15

I   **Basic Boston & Albany** 18

        A Short History
        "Wooden Cars and Iron Men" by Lewis H. Bullard
        "Memories of the Boston & Albany" by Stanley H. Smith
        "The Last Two Decades of B&A Steam" by Brian R. Scace

II   **Boston: The Road's Anchor** 39

        South Station to Beacon Park
        "Yards and Engines" by Paul T. Carver
        Grand Junction Branch
        "Remembering the Grand Junction" by Preston Johnson

III   **Outbound to Framingham** 77

        The Commuter District
        Highland Branch
        Newton Lower Falls Branch
        Saxonville Branch
        Milford Branch

IV   **Over the Hill to Worcester** 117

        Main Line Running
        "New York City Trains"
        "Dining Aboard"
        Millbury Branch
        "Carrying the Mail" by Brian R. Scace
        "Onboard a Railway Post Office" by Frank X. Lundy

Bibliography and Index . . . . Volume II: Worcester to Albany

FOREWORD

Robert A. Buck

My friend Stanley Smith, who was 82 when we met, always called it the "Albany." To him the Boston & Albany was a big, brawny, high-rolling railroad with connections to far away places. He loved the Boston & Maine and the New Haven, and spent part of his youth as a motorman on the Middlesex & Boston. But his highest regard was for the "Albany," where he'd briefly been a baggage handler. When he'd visit, I'd get him a chair since he was so frail, and he'd lean on his cane and reminisce. In his youth he saw some of the heaviest 4-4-0 Americans built by Schenectedy come to the B&A in 1900, Atlantics in 1902, and Pacifics in 1903. The B&A had big stuff, even in those days.

For myself, I got hooked early on the B&A, from about age three when I first reached the window sill of this house, where I still live. The view was down toward the Warren town common, just adjacent to the railroad. Without knowing what they were, I saw the articulateds, and I grew up watching fascinating things on the B&A such as the *Royal Scot*, whose engineer waved at me, and whose beautiful loco was the London-Midland-Scottish No. 6100, in America for the Chicago Century of Progress in 1933.

In 1934 I went down to the station in Mother's care and watched the *Zephyr* come through, making its early tour over the B&A to Boston, even before it got to Colorado. It went from the Budd Company's Red Lion shops outside Philadelphia right up the eastern seaboard. And what showmanship! The train was visited by an incredible number of people before it ever got to Burlington land.

It was about 1935 that I experienced my first train ride, on B&A train 30, from Springfield to Warren. I didn't ride often until later years when we went to Boston a great deal. My grandparents lived in Greenville, Maine, and Grandfather carried the mail between Greenville and Greenville Junction, from the post office to the trains. At Greenville Junction he showed me the regal Canadian Pacific with its line across Maine, and the Bangor and Aroostook—the *other* B&A.

The Rexall Train came through in 1937, and The *City of Salina*—that ugly Union Pacific thing—also came by once. The *Coronation Scot* passed through in 1939 on its way to the New York World's Fair. My Dad and a friend got our station agent to come down and turn the station lights on about 9:00 p.m. when it was due eastbound. In the late sixties Alan Pegler brought the *Flying Scotsman* from England. It was unloaded in Boston and ran over the B&A. We wanted to hear what a three-cylinder would sound like working full out, so we went over to Charlton Hill which was the only place it would be working hard before Anniston, Alabama. God, what a sound!

Other interesting visitors were the demonstrator engines from Alco, EMD, and Fairbanks-Morse. In those years the B&A was host to special trains of Truman, Wilkie, and Dewey, and I even saw Alfred Landon's train with a big sunflower on the back of the Pullman.

The B&A is not as well known in New England as the Boston & Maine or the New Haven, and I have felt in the minority of fans. All my friends were scooped up by one or the other, while here was this railroad in the middle, running between the two, looked upon with some disdain because it was owned by "outlanders." But it really was the big gun with the great steel fleet, with trains like the *Twentieth Century's* Boston section, later called the *New England States*, the *Paul Revere*, *North Shore Limited*, the *Ohio State Limited*, the *Iroquois*, the *Knickerbocker*, the *Wolverine*, and the *Southwestern Limited*.

Although the railroad was sometimes perceived as "foreign-owned," with suggestions of aloof management, the B&A's people identified more with that railroad name than they did with the New York Central. Our agent in Warren was Jack Conway for many years, a friendly person who kept us informed whenever we'd go down and inquire. He was the passenger agent, ticket seller, operator when required, and freight clerk too. After World War II, with so many station closures, we had a procession of agents as one bumped another on the seniority list. Still, Warren did remain open until the late 1950s, unlike Hinsdale which closed in 1937. It was local industry that kept Warren active in later times, especially Warren Steam Pump Company which produced so much Navy shipping material during the war.

The scale of railroading was so different then. Today the public is much less aware of the railroads. But my childhood saw them still vital to much of rural America, when almost everyone knew someone who worked for the railroad.

Warren was a very typical small town. It had a fair number of local sidings, all gone today. We had the Fanny Jane Woolen Mill where the siding was used mostly for coal, and right in the middle of town was a coal and grain company into whose sheds the coal was sorted into various grades. Adjacent was a team track for miscellaneous loading. A thousand feet west was the freight house with its platform track extending into a lumber yard. At the turn of the century there was a siding into Perkins Machine Co. (formerly the Slater Engine Co., maker of stationary steam engines), and right across from the B&A passenger station, swinging off and going due south up a

Above: In the golden lushness of summer on June 12, 1966, the eastbound New England States passes the Sun Valley siding at Warren behind a pair of E-8s. Robert A. Buck photo. *Below:* The last steam run on the Boston & Albany enters Worcester Union Station on Monday, April 16, 1951. NYC 4-8-2 No. 3004 does the proud honors this day at the head of the westbound Wolverine. Oscar V. Payne photo/Stephen R. Payne collection.

Foreword

Left: *The original Western Railroad station at Chester as seen on August 20, 1988. This view looks to the west. The building has since been moved to the north side of the tracks to help ensure its preservation. Brian Solomon photo.*

Right: *The famous* Flying Scotsman *is climbing Charlton Hill in 1969, westbound for New York City. The handsome, three-cylinder locomotive was magnificently painted in the black and green of the London & North Eastern Railway. Robert A. Buck photo from October 1969.*

hellish grade, was a commercial siding to the Knowles Pump Co.

The house track east of the Warren Pumps was about a half mile long. In my time it came into town and had a very short passing siding—a holdover of the third tracks put in about 1912 in several locations to relieve congestion around severe grades. This was done at State Line Tunnel, North Adams Junction to Hinsdale, Springfield Hill, Charlton Hill, and West Warren to Warren.

Almost anywhere you went on the B&A would find an arrangement similar to Warren's. At nearby West Brookfield, for example, there was a coal yard, a yeast mill, a lumber yard, and big team tracks. World War II breathed the last great life into New England industry, most of it gone today.

As with so many who love a particular railroad, it was my early association with the B&A that sparked my intense interest—really it's not to strong to say *love* for it. Then, too, it was a *big-time* railroad. It had literally the very latest modern steam power—Pacifics, Mikes, Berkshires, and Hudsons—that set it way ahead of neighboring roads. Even the branches were heavy duty, laid with rail from the main lines that had been replaced. And the Consolidations, which we usually think of as tea kettle engines, were the big, fat-boilered Central design.

Probably everyone has one special train experience that stands above the rest. Mine was the *Wolverine* on April 15, 1951, pulled by NYC Mohawk 3004, the last steam to run officially on the B&A. I was going to do my best to capture it on film. I called the B&A dispatcher and said, "I know you can't stop that train in Warren, but would you put a message out for it to give one long whistle through town?" A very small group of us stood with cameras ready on the south side of the tracks across from the station. It was gray, misty, and not very nice. The train's arrival coincided with the last of the day's light, so photos were not very successful. She was all painted up with white striping on the drivers and running boards, something I had never seen before on the B&A. Her very unusual, not particularly melodious whistle was screaming its last good-bye. This is a special memory. A grand triumph of B&A steam.

Years later I used the *Wolverine* when they were cutting back on passenger service. Warren had been eliminated as a stop and Palmer was being thinned down. One compromise offered Palmer was to stop Train 33 there after they took off the local Budd Car. That was great. I would drive 15 minutes to Palmer, take an eastbound and do business in Boston, come out on 33 and have the joy of eating in the dining car. It was an extra treat I looked forward to.

Another fellow and I used to cover the B&A very thoroughly, especially in the war years, sometime before I had gotten an automobile or learned to drive, and I remember being permitted to go down to Palmer by my parents for the entire day of July 4, 1945, with camera to see a Sports model 1400 [2-8-4 Berkshire] whaling across the diamond with a troop train. This was a day when one could go down and see the Ware River Branch, some of the activity of the CV crossing the B&A, local freights out

from both Worcester and Springfield, a fair number of passenger trains, expresses, lowly locals, and the works. I stayed until 5:00 p.m. and got a good overview of the activity.

I would always hear crews speaking of "the West End," but didn't discover it myself until 1946. I drove grandmother's 1937 Packard, using almost equal amounts of gas and oil, but it got us there. A good friend, Warren St. George, and I watched the parade. We followed a freight out through Woronoco to Huntington to Chester, watched them put a Mike on the front, a second one on the back, and up the hill they went. Later on we got over to North Adams Junction, over to Hinsdale to what looked like an incredible grade dropping off. By early afternoon it was raining, and train 49, the *Knickerbocker* came up with ten cars and a NYC 3100 Mohawk, unassisted. That was quite a feat, to go up that hill without a helper. We got the 1416 Berkshire a few minutes later, on its hands and knees, with a 1200 Mike behind, and 46 cars. Clawing at the hill, slipping, grabbing it again—and they made it— but it was quite a performance to watch.

We later met an engineer whom we came to like quite well, Louie Blanchard, one of three Blanchards working on the B&A. All were Chester men, so generally they were in helper service. Louis later became a mainline man, running train 93 which normally had Pacifics, later RS's, and once in a while one of those awful Baldwin "Gravel Gerties." They were useless for almost anything besides a local. The steam heat didn't work, but since you didn't need it in the summer anyway, they were chosen. Louie was the first man we met on a Budd Car. "Wait'll we get out on the flats at Wilbraham. Show ya what it'll do!" And he did, and he brought it up to 81 mph. He said "the automatic governor cuts out at 83 so we'll keep it under there." We were quite impressed by the speed. One day Superintendent A. M. Scott came up and said, "Louie, I hope you'll give us a good push today." Louie told him, "I'll give you a *fair* push. I give everybody a *fair* push. No more. No less!"

One day I was joined in my store by three of my favorite old-timers: Stuart Woolley, an engineer friend, was 81; Albert Smith, a retired agent, was 96; and newly retired was Ralph Tobin, whose father was also an agent at Barre Plains for many years. Of course we were soon talking about the old days and I spoke of the conductor on train 93. Dropping his name I said, "I bet you guys knew him." Albert glowered at me. "Yes, the son-of-bitch," and we were off. It seems Albert asked this fellow to take care of his son, expecting free passage, back when such courtesies were common if not officially sanctioned. "He took care of him all right," Albert snarled, "he charged him full fare!" Stuart explained that the conductor was once pinched by a spotter and vowed never to be caught again, even if it was his grandmother riding.

Stuart finally admitted the truth to one story which I'd heard for a long time. Seems he was on the Springfield station switcher one hot, muggy summer's night, just washing down the deck with a hose waiting for the next assignment when the *Iroquois* came rolling in. Most of the windows were open this hot night and, as the train passed

by, here was this well-rounded pink fanny in a open Pullman window. So naturally he gave her a squirt. "Why," he said, "you've never heard such screaming and yelling in that station. We had to take the engine up back of the freight house."

They remembered other, older engineers who always used to crab about the 1300-series articulated compounds. You couldn't run them over 30 mph or they'd crack their frames. Stuart Woolley also referred to the very early cross-compounds on the B&A. They had some 4-8-0s and a few 0-6-0s and two regal looking, high-wheeled ten-wheelers, the 220 and 221. Apparently they all were rebuilt into simple engines. They had a high pressure cylinder on the left and a low pressure one on the right, and they were nick-named "Slam-Bangs."

The B&A was very innovative. This was a railroad that experimented and then purchased new types of motive power and equipment. Five high-hood diesels, HH600s, came on the property in 1939, with Beacon Park as their stomping ground. They were the only diesels ever to receive B&A lettering. My friend Charles A. Brown had a photo of NYC Box Cab three-power, oil battery electrics working the Exeter Street coach yard in 1937—very strange and unusual creatures these.

The B&A today still has much of its old flavor, even with all that's been lost. Much as we still have the legacy of Pennsylvania's Horseshoe Curve, or the New York Central's Great Water Level Route, you can hike up in the Berkshires and it is *still* the Boston & Albany. The vestiges are there—the deep rock cuts; the Twin Ledges at Middlefield; the cuttings along the Westfield River; the original Western Railroad station at Chester (now preserved on the north side of the tracks); at West Brookfield both the original Western Railroad passenger station and freight house still stand; the Whistler Arches, even the massive piles of cinders along the right-of-way left there by Winans Mud Diggers and Eddy Clocks and Articulateds and Hudsons and Berkshires—these just yell out Boston & Albany to you.

On an early 1950s day rich with saturated green and blue, the westbound Knickerbocker *has just passed through Turtle Bend, just west of Russell. On the point is NYC RS-3 No. 8314 with a sister unit, two express cars, and six passenger cars. Thomas J. McNamara photo.*

ACKNOWLEDGEMENTS

I have been having the time of my life writing this book. Such a good time, in fact, that the project has resisted closure for much too long. I found the subject so large and absorbing that it merited two volumes. In many instances, photography was more difficult to come by than in my two earlier books. And my decision to include numerous personal interviews caused several months' delay. Now, in expressing thanks to those who have participated, I am deeply grateful to those who lent me photographs for the book. Some of these patient souls have been waiting three years for the return of their slides, probably wondering if perhaps I and the photographs were abducted by aliens (very interesting experience, actually. It seems these saucer types are actually able to restore discolored Ektachromes). To these people I owe the most thanks, because their images power this book.

A hearty round of applause for the 39 photographers:

Howard Ande	D. Robert McCulloch
Jack Armstrong	John Morrison
David C. Bartlett	Russell F. Munroe
Robert A. Buck	Leon Onofri
Norton D. Clark	Oscar Payne
William T. Clynes	Stephen R. Payne
Stanley W. Cook	Ben Perry
F. Rodney Dirkes	Donald S. Robinson
T. J. Donahue	Richard B. Sanborn
William G. Dulmaine, Jr.	Dave Santos
George E. Ford, Jr.	Jim Shaughnessy
Richard B. Gassett	Stanley H. Smith
Scott Hartley	Brian Solomon
Lawson K. Hill	Richard Jay Solomon
Wayne D. Hills	Carl H. Sturner
Brian L. Jennison	Jack Trowill
John F. Kane	George W. Turnbull
Jim Lang	John M. Wallace
Thomas J. McNamara	Allan H. Wiswall
Fred H. Matthews	

I have made many wonderful new friends in writing about the Boston & Albany. I thank my own "Big Four" for the primary inspiration in telling the B&A story: Robert A. Buck, Paul Carver, Brian Scace, and Brian Solomon. I speak more about their contributions in the *Introduction* on the opposite page. Suffice it to say here that I leaned on them heavily and repeatedly for information, photography, and advice.

Also especially helpful was Richard U. Cogswell, Jr. He sent stories from RAILWAY AGE that were not easily accessible, copies of several key historical documents relating to South Station, and he reviewed and offered suggestions for the South Station chapter.

Rick Hurst of Amtrak's Boston Division Commuter Service provided various facts and figures about its present-day operation, including track charts of South Station which were invaluable. John Baesch, who served there for several years as Assistant General Superintendant—Commuter, similarly provided charts and data along with colorful anecdotes.

Railroad paper can be a fine visual treat, and I am indebted to Jack May, William D. Clynes, and Preston Johnson for lending me numerous B&A tickets, timetables, and maps. Through Michael Sullivan I was able to purchase a portion of Warren Jacobs's B&A collection, which included a number of tickets. Mike also graciously permitted his excellent B&A china to be photographed for the book. Howard Moulton provided much useful information about Railway Post Office cars, and he gave me several examples of RPO paper to use.

My sister, Pamela Jones Aamodt, has created another set of wonderful illustrations for the chapter-heads. My friends at Pentrex again helped with the book; Katie Danneman designed the cover, Paul Hammond made many cogent suggestions about fine-tuning the layout, and Dean Sauvola executed the South Station track charts with great care.

Three important photographic collections are represented, those of Norton D. Clark, Leon Onofri, and Stanley H. Smith. I thank Skip Clark's widow, Susan, and their son, Lonnie, for their generous assistance in making the photographs available. Annette and Joe Onofri have given me unlimited access to their late father's extensive collection, encouraging publication. And E. James Gibbons has been very forthcoming with his slide collection of the late Stanley H. Smith.

A special thanks to Ben Perry who provided more than a hundred slides covering dozens of locations which I would not have otherwise found. Likewise, Kevin Farrell lent me many fascinating black & white B&A photos from the turn of the century. Charles Bahne helped with details about stations in the Boston area, James Wilkie was a knowledgeable source in dating several black & while photos, and Bob McCulloch was unstinting with his time in helping to answer technical questions, particularly on the west end. Peter T. Victory spent many hours helping with research, especially on the Grand Junction Branch.

Scott Logan at Complete Color in Glendale, California, has brought great artistry to the color restoration work in the slides. Mac Sebree once again gave valuable time for proofreading, as did Rick Welles who also assisted with measurements at South Station. Finally I express my appreciation to Thomas J. Humphrey, an expert railroad historian from Newton, Massachusetts, who came to my aid at the eleventh hour, offering advice and making numerous factual corrections in the text.

My grateful thanks to you all.

INTRODUCTION

It is worth remembering that the Boston & Albany existed only for 33 years as an independent body. It was born with the combining of the Boston & Worcester and Western Railroads in 1867, and it died—in fact if not in mind—in 1900 with its absorption into the New York Central. Had fate been otherwise, the mighty NYC might have been owned by the B&A, but Boston financiers shied from the risk and New York City did the honors. But 97 years after its acquisition by the NYC, the B&A name still lingers on tongues today. Conrail dispatchers and train operators still speak of this track as Boston & Albany. While all Boston's other commuter rail lines—former B&M and New Haven—are dispatched by the MBTA, this famous line west is dispatched by Conrail. The restoration of Boston-Worcester commuter service (along with the second track so shortsightedly ripped up in the early 1980s) and Boston's continuing growth as an intermodal port bode well for the continued prosperity of the line.

We have all experienced the vivid intensity of childhood memories. A child's impressions are colored by logic only at some later age. My childhood memories of the New Haven Railroad were of the shining streamlined coaches at South Station, while memories of the Boston & Albany were more elusive. One recurs of a night in the fifties when my Dad and I walked from his Federal Building office in Post Office Square out to the Sheraton Plaza in Copley Square for dinner. Later that balmy summer evening we walked to a movie house to see Alec Guiness in *The Lavender Hill Mob*. Up Boylston Street we went, past the B&A passenger yard which swept away from the street like a silvery spider web (see photo on page 63). Today you'd hardly know that a railroad ever ran here, for the yard's land is occupied by the Prudential Center, recently renewed after two decades' wallow into seediness. The B&A right-of-way is shared with the Massachusetts Turnpike in a tunnel.

On that darkening night, this end of town was quiet, even enervated, and the lights from the dwarf signals and semaphores glinted faintly in the dimness. Dad and I stopped on the bridge over the mainline to look down at the yard. No trains came, the rush hour having expended itself an hour earlier, so we walked on to our movie.

My impressions that night color my childhood memories of the B&A. I always thought of it as a railroad at dusk with a faint semaphore light peering through swirling night, and black-green coaches. This memory of darkness was reinforced during my freshman year in high school when I and three dozen fellow students went by bus one Saturday to John Hancock Hall for the New England Drama Festival sponsored by the Boston Globe. The first play was in the morning and the festival lasted well into the evening.

After dinner, as a respite from the long day of play watching, I took my No. 116 bellows camera and walked a couple of blocks to the subterranean bliss of Back Bay Station. Though it was indeed very dark, I walked a ways on the tracks—a couple of blocks—toward South Station, and it soon became apparent how the tracks of the B&A and those of the New Haven diverged here. The two rights-of-way were separated by a long, large stone wall, with half-moon openings every few feet. Through them I saw flashes of a loud, growling diesel. It may have been a switcher on its way to the passenger yard or the freight facility at Beacon Park. Maybe it was a mail train going west. Yet my impression was of great age, old machinery, deliberate, mysterious late-night movement, unknowable destinations. I didn't realize that I could have gone up to the street and come down into either one of the B&A stations—Huntington Avenue or Trinity Place—two massive granite stations, one serving outbound-, the other inbound traffic. So this night I stayed on the New Haven side.

After college I worked for the Opera Company of Boston for a season. I lived on Westland Avenue in "The Alice," a slightly down-at-the-heels building owned by the Christian Science Church, in a $90-a-month apartment with a trash barrel view of the alley, half a block from Symphony Hall. I walked to work at 172 Newbury Street by going up Massachusetts Avenue, where I could see the B&A tracks just before they led into the Prudential Center tunnel. Oftentimes I'd see the morning commuter train from Framingham—usually ten or so "turtle-back" coaches in a bleached dark green—pulled by a very noisy New York Central E-7. Perhaps it was in Penn Central dress; I only remember how shabby it looked.

Unlike the Boston & Maine with its sprawling labyrinth clutching all upper New England, or the New Haven with its colorful stable of New York City trains, to my young eyes the Boston & Albany had a singular approach to railroading. It had one mainline, going west, and one could ride it to Chicago.

It is rather fitting that it is in such good shape today. It was one of the three earliest railroads in New England, having opened as the Boston & Worcester in July 1835. As the Conrail mainline, it's the most economically viable in today's unstable Northeast rail market. The Boston & Albany was not the lure the Boston & Maine was to me as a boy. Yet in the intervening years my fascination with the B&A has intensified dramatically.

My mother's Uncle Jack visited us a few times when we were kids. After one visit in 1955, Dad drove us all from Marblehead to Boston to drop Uncle Jack at South Station for his trip home to Berwick, Pennsylvania. He worked there as a passenger car estimator for American

Car & Foundry (he told us that streamlined cars cost $100,000). We encountered a major traffic snarl in the Sumner Tunnel (its single lane in either direction made this a frequent occurrence). Even with extra time planned, we were late to the station, and Jack missed his 8:00 p.m. train. He had to wait for a 10:00 or 11:00 departure. He had reserved a room, and changing reservations at that late hour could not have been easy.

This trip was my first to South Station. It was a big place and it was very, very busy. The concourse was high and bright—many lights—many bustling people—children with parents—the din of moving travelers—lines of taxis at the curving front arcade—newspapers, cigarettes, candies, magazines for sale—porters, red-caps, suitcases everywhere—and of course shoeshine stands. With all this activity, two things stood out for a child: the little photo booths with their instant pictures, and the souvenir coin stamping machines. For a quarter you could stamp your choice of up to 12 letters on the coin-with-spokes which popped out of the machine. Uncle Jack gave me the quarter but I messed up and it came out "Maqblehead." I kept it for years.

While in high school, my friend Lincoln Soule and I often explored trains in Boston on Saturdays and school holidays. These trips occasionally took us to South Station where we found the equipment to be far more varied than the Budd Cars and the *Talgo* at North Station. South Station had a lot of colorful New Haven equipment. We saw a Pennsy train, *The Senator*, and New York Central Budd Cars—called *Beeliners*—which handled a daily Albany train. We rarely saw the Framingham commuter because it didn't operate weekends. For years I assumed that B&A trains used only the low-numbered tracks in the depot, yet the one time I saw the *New England States* arrive, as I stood out by Tower No. 1, it berthed in one of the center tracks. In my memory (and one photo) the train consists of smooth-sided, two-tone gray cars, all dirty (probably there were streamlined cars at the front). For me, South Station's real glory was its bridge rows of red semaphore blades high above the tracks. These were part of the original 1899 signal equipment which lasted into the 1970s. Their years of service were a testimony to the durability of their design. I suppose they had to go sooner or later but, my, they were regal beings.

At South Station the baggage, mail, and express wagons had access to the platforms via a series of subterranean tunnels which emerged onto the platforms far away from the concourse (North Station, by contrast, had ramps that came down from above). There was a series of Railway Express tracks, off to the west side of the station tracks, where head-end express cars were serviced.

The waiting room at South Station was huge. It had classic, straight-backed wooden benches, perfectly suitable for visiting parsons and their issue. The ceiling was very high and there were large windows high on the walls. The concourse was long and broad with a restaurant and a big newsstand in the middle.

B&A trains departed from the low-numbered tracks at South Station—Track 1 being at the far right as one faced them from the concourse. Most B&A trains used the first eight tracks, with long trains assigned, variously over the years, to tracks 12, 13, and 14, the station's longest. The reason for using the low-numbered tracks was one of efficiency. All movements from the main line and Exeter Street yard—where cars were stored and diners restocked at the commissary—were most efficiently handled on the northwest three of the eight tracks running between South Station and Back Bay.

When my first book, about the Boston & Maine, was published in 1990, I included a first chapter disgorging every fact I could remember from my boyhood growing up around the B&M. I couldn't do that in my second book, about Vermont's railroads, because I didn't grow up in Vermont. Yet I have felt, since the latter's publication in 1994, that it lacked the personal dimension of the B&M book. In conceiving these two volumes about the B&A, beyond finding high-quality color photography, I have relied on others' words to acquaint the reader with the Boston & Albany. Beginning with Robert A. Buck's *Foreword* we have a taste of what the B&A was like in mid-twentieth century. Bob is a keen observer of the B&A and has watched it some six decades. Along the way he handed the torch to the much younger Brian Solomon who has given us his own perspective on today's B&A in the *Epilogue* in Volume II, along with a number of his especially powerful photographs. Brian is among the most talented rail photographers active today.

For technical information I have relied most strongly on two friends, Brian Scace and Paul Carver. Brian's detailed piece on modern B&A steam was first seen in the New York Central System Historical Society's fine magazine, CENTRAL HEADLIGHT, and has been reworked by him for inclusion here. Brian assiduously separates the wheat from the chaff, and has been a great help in discerning lore from fact. I have especially enjoyed his account of the eastbound *Lake Shore* from Albany in "Riding the Mountain" in Volume II. Paul Carver is a veritable encyclopedia of rail facts, his technical assistance being of special note, and his editing skills were applied most usefully to several drafts of the manuscript.

For an earlier B&A, I turned to two older written accounts. Lewis H. Bullard's *Wooden Cars and Iron Men* appeared (under a different title) in the May-June 1941 issue of THE RAILROAD ENTHUSIAST; its recall of detail is astonishing. It is a compelling portrait of railroading at the turn of the century. Stanley H. Smith's reminiscences of one decade later are equally rich and fascinating. Smith handed out his recollections to friends in typescript, though I don't believe the material has received actual publication prior to this book. Late in his life Smith turned to color photography; several of his pictures grace these pages.

Looking further for the *feel* of railroading, I interviewed men who worked on the B&A. Clarence Gardner worked as a fireman while steam engines still plied the North Adams Branch. Robert Roche's descriptions of the nuts-and-bolts of being a freight conductor are full of detail, told very much from the professional railroader's point of view (both in Volume II)

My friend Preston Johnson, who served 44 years on the Boston & Maine—34 of them as a dispatcher—was a gold mine of information about the B&A's Grand Junction Branch; he worked right alongside it for a time. His "Remembering the Grand Junction" is full of wonderful facts. Preston is one of those rare railroaders who kept copious records of his work activities—a great boon to the rail historian. I was so impressed with Frank X. Lundy's interview in Stuart Leuthner's seminal *The Railroaders* (if you don't have it you should) about working on New York Central RPO cars, that I phoned him in Florida to learn more about his B&A beginnings. This, together with Brian Scace's "Carrying the Mail," is of particular interest to anyone fascinated, as I am, about how the railroads conveyed U. S. Mail.

I've known Bill Dulmaine for years, the editor of the New Haven Railroad Historical and Technical Association's beautiful SHORELINER magazine. But only by chance did I discover that his high school years were spent living adjacent to the Millbury Branch; his opening anecdote is colorful indeed.

Mac Sebree, onetime Publisher at Interurban press, is a writer with a uniquely deft touch. He learned his craft as a reporter for United Press International where brevity was tempered with the occasional tart turn of phrase. His "Telegraph Interlude" in the second volume shows what a good storyteller he is. Mac's pleasure in writing will communicate to you immediately.

The Reverend Walter H. Smith was kind enough to share his writing about his father's experience as a crossing tender on the Ware River Branch—remember when there were crossing tenders practically everywhere?

In the autumn of 1995 I interviewed two veterans of the B&A Extra Board. Andy Paine fired steam locomotives in 1944 before joining the army, and will quickly engage you with his salty wartime experiences. Station and tower agent Robert Gardner held assignments in 33 different locations during his compact 12-year tenure. He was on duty at Woronoco when the *Lake Shore Limited* nearly went into the Westfield River after a 1955 washout. Then for a narrative about a typical afternoon trick in B&A's Tower 66 in Chatham, you'll enjoy Bob McCulloch's observations about the interesting activity there 40 years ago.

I love to quote what people have to say about railroads, and I've stuck quotations in anywhere I thought they added color. I wanted to make an evocative book about the B&A with strong photography and vivid prose, and I'm indebted to those men who talked directly with me, and to those who left behind written accounts that have fit nicely with our plan.

The mountainous terrain of western Massachusetts has bred many hardy railroaders who collectively inspired our chapter called *Railroad Life in the Berkshires*. William Gregor Ryan of Pittsfield recalls his days as a yardmaster, and we have some letters between Pittsfield agent Frank E. Leonard and a NYC auditor which will cheer anyone who has ever endured bureaucratic scrutiny. Especially I want you to know about the woman named Nellie MacDonald, whose story I stumbled across while fleshing out what it was like being a country station agent. She touched my heart, and I think she will touch yours.

Our little group of writers and photographers has been laboring just about a century to bring you this collection of photos, illustrations, facts, reminiscences, conjectures, and sundry memorabilia about the Boston & Albany. It's a terrific story. May you have as much pleasure roaming about the two volumes of this book as we have had in creating them.

Robert Willoughy Jones
Silverlake
Los Angeles, California
November 1996

This stone arch bridge in Middlefield was one of nine built on the Western Railroad's original 1841 alignment, engineered by Major George Washington Whistler. A realignment in 1912 made them obsolete; three survive, unused, while a fourth was strengthened and is used by Conrail. Late 1940s photo, Leon Onofri collection.

I

BASIC BOSTON & ALBANY
A Short History

The railroad became an ever more visible presence on the landscape. Six railroad causeways and eight railroad terminals were now headquartered at the Hub. Some eighty-three train stations inflated the radial towns into "railroad villages." The power of the steam engine astounded everyone. The railroad's "terrible energy" fascinated Hawthorne, unfixing every corner of the country from its age-long rest, he wrote. Even Thoreau who felt dismay at hearing the "hills echo with its snort-like thunder" admitted that he felt "as if the earth had got a race now worthy to inhabit it." Incredulous Bostonians watched the old farms and graceful estates around the city begin to take on village airs while even remote spots like Lowell, Worcester, and Salem seemed "almost suburbs" to their inhabitants. "From the moment that railways were introduced, life took on extravagance," Henry Adams wrote.

Land values multiplied in the railroad's trail. The path of the iron horse appeared to be the route to real estate development and commercial boom. No wonder Bostonians saw the railroad station at South Cove, not the harbor, as the gateway to the town. The city's very prosperity seemed to ride upon the rails. The capital from commerce and manufacturing went to fund the new locomotives. Boston banks and bankers bolstered the system as it spread across the continent. The link with the western routes from Boston to Canada foretold golden days to come. Progress was on every hand, symbolized in so many things—in the new steamers that docked from Liverpool, in the telegraph messages from across the sea, in the prosperous factories and flourishing land development.

Jane Holtz Kay
LOST BOSTON (1980)

The Boston & Albany was created September 4, 1867, the combining of the Boston & Worcester and Western Railroads. Before citing the political obstacles which delayed the merger from happening 25 years earlier, let us consider the economic forces calling for the building of railroads in Massachusetts in the early 1800s.

Boston had been the focus of shipbuilding and overseas commerce since the arrival of John Winthrop and his group of settlers in 1630. The plentiful cod in Massachusetts Bay helped build fortunes as the dried fish was shipped to the West Indies, where it was fed to the African slaves working the British-owned sugar plantations. Soon Boston found eager buyers among the Roman Catholic citizenry of the Mediterranean. The Puritans vilified the Pope but they gladly profited from his denial of meat on Fridays. The city's other exports were flour, dried beef, and barrel staves, while its imports were wine, sugar, molasses, and gold. Of all British ports, Boston ranked only third behind London and Bristol by 1700. The city went into a slump following the Revolutionary War when it lost its British markets, then rebounded with the growth of trade with the Far East. The War of 1812 nearly ruined Boston's sea trade. President Thomas Jefferson and Congress had imposed a trade embargo with the British in 1807. Then the British blockaded American ports, severely blunting Boston's role as the leading trade center in America.

The city never recovered its maritime pre-eminence after the War of 1812. Capital once invested in shipping now went into textiles. By contrast, New York City sensed early on that the next important era was to be trade with the interior, especially to the west. Men began to envision how to move goods more efficiently than by the circuitous rivers and poor roads.

Massachusetts' rugged terrain posed barriers to roads and canals, and it soon lost out to New York when the Erie Canal opened in 1825. New York now had an all-water route up the Hudson as far west as the Great Lakes. Boston money was eager to catch up. First a canal from Boston to the Connecticut River was proposed in 1825 by a committee of the Legislature. The idea quickly escalated into the concept of a canal all the way to Albany.

There were three distinct geographic regions along a southern route across Massachusetts, each with differing business profiles, and each with different transportation needs. Worcester County, settled in 1731, had a modest agriculture which lost out to New York and states further west. It later found success in textiles with the abundant local water power (66 woolen mills in Worcester in 1837). Worcester excelled in metal working, producing farm implements, firearms, wire, and shoes. The city needed better transportation to get these products to the densely populated Boston area. The 1828 Blackstone Canal, effecting water travel to Providence, was frozen at least four months in the winter and was thus only a partial solution.

Springfield's fertile Connecticut River Valley was first settled in 1635. Cotton mills started about 1825 while woolen mills came later. Power for the mills in the valley came from the Chicopee, Ware, Miller's, Westfield, and Deerfield Rivers. Most commerce went south down the Connecticut River. Yet even after the Farmington Canal opened to New Haven in 1830 and to Northampton in 1835, the textile alliance with Boston was still strong, and crying out for improved transportation.

The Berkshire Hills isolated western Massachusetts. Settlement there was late, in 1744, and its farming failed about 1800 with the competition from New York. The population declined after 1810, then grew again from 1830 as marble, granite, iron, paper, and textiles drew investors' attention. Still, the lack of transportation slowed industrial development.

Throughout Massachusetts, turnpikes were not effective alternatives for shipping manufactured goods. Overland travel from Boston to Albany via Worcester, Springfield, and Pittsfield worked only for passengers and mail.

A serendipitous event then occurred in Massachusetts which quickly altered thinking about a canal. The cornerstone of Bunker Hill Monument was laid June 17, 1825. Gridley Bryant, the contractor supplying the stone, was aware of early English horsepower railroads. Imagining that such a conveyance could move the granite from his quarry in Quincy three miles to water where he could ship it across the harbor by boat, he built what came to be known as the Quincy Granite Railway. Many consider this to be the first incorporated railroad in America. Concurrently the rapid, successful development of rail in England was watched with great interest by American capitalists, many of whom looked askance at the idea of a cross-Massachusetts canal. Particularly irksome was the idea that the canal was only possible if a five-mile tunnel were bored through the formidable Hoosac Mountain.

A nasty debate raged from 1827 to 1831 over whether the railroad should be built with public or private money. Even strong backers doubted whether it could pay interest on its cost. Capitalists, looking to minimize risk, naturally lobbied on behalf of subsidy from the Massachusetts Legislature. Opposed were farmers and local governments who envisioned higher taxes and possible loss of local commerce. Particularly vulnerable were towns not situated on a proposed line.

One especially ardent advocate of the railroad was Nathan Hale of the *Boston Advertiser*. He addressed specifically how the railroads would benefit each economic group in Massachusetts: the farmers in the Connecticut Valley; Springfield industry; and Boston mercantile interests. Industrialists began to be convinced. Governor Lincoln threw his support to the railroad in 1827 and finally that year the Legislature authorized two commissioners, an engineer, and $10,000 to study two routes.

A new Board of Internal Improvements made a report on January 16, 1829, recommending the building of railroads to Albany and Providence. For the former, a southern route via Framingham, Worcester, Springfield, Pittsfield, and West Stockbridge was proposed as less costly than a route to the north. But the question was still red hot and, when the Board recommended the state borrow $3 million to finance the road, this became the central issue of the 1829 state election.

In 1829 the Legislature rejected a bill for a state-supported railway between Boston and Albany. With this defeat, private interests organized among themselves. In 1830 and 1831, the State received charter applications for the Boston & Lowell, Boston & Providence, and Boston & Worcester Railroads. Demonstrating the lightning speed with which railroad fever gripped Massachusetts, all three opened to their destinations in a nine-week period in 1835, just five years after the Baltimore & Ohio opened as America's first common carrier.

The Boston & Worcester Railroad

The charter of the Boston & Worcester was a compromise, a disappointment for the visionaries who believed that Albany should be reached sooner rather than later. But such a huge a project frightened many, in part because the potential for cost overruns was so high. The charter included a clause prohibiting for 30 years any competing line between Boston, Brookline, Cambridge, or Charlestown to Worcester. Its purpose was to protect the investment, but its ultimate effect was to thwart the combination of the Boston & Worcester with its soon-to-be born companion to the west, the Western Railroad.

Financing the construction of the Boston & Worcester proceeded slowly; subscriptions were slow in being paid. When work finally began in August 1832, the track was built cheaply. By using sharp curves the engineers needed fewer deep cuts. Still, crossing the hilly terrain to

> **From *Report of the Directors to the Stockholders 1832 Boston & Worcester R. R.***
>
> "A person was employed to make an enumeration of the carriages and wagons which passed Kimball's tavern in Needham, at the point where the Hopkinton road and Worcester turnpike diverge from each other; supposed to be coming to and going from Boston, during the month of October 1831; this enumeration gave the following results:
>
> | | |
> |---|---|
> | Chaises | 1069 |
> | Carry alls | 300 |
> | 1-horse wagon | 1199 |
> | 2-horse wagon | 626 |
> | 3-horse wagon | 239 |
> | 4-horse wagon | 524 |
> | 5-horse wagon | 292 |
> | 6-horse wagon | 296 |
> | 7-horse wagon | 114 |
> | 8-horse wagon | 63 |
> | Ox teams | 596 |
> | Stages drawn by 4 horses | 413 |
>
> "The enumeration did not distinguish, as was intended, the number which passed the Hopkinton road from those which passed the Worcester Turnpike."

Worcester necessitated a climb of 503 feet. The B&W operated the first steam train in New England, from Boston to Newton, on April 7, 1834. The first steam locomotive built in New England, *The Yankee*, was one of the B&W's first four locomotives. The others—*The Meteor*, *The Comet*, and *The Rocket*—were constructed in England between 1834 and 1835 at the Stephenson works at Newcastle-on-Tyne.

Not everyone wanted the railroad. A strong turnpike lobby in the Legislature was sympathetic to the plight of the stagecoach companies which were clearly about to lose their business. Landowner opposition in Framingham Center forced the routing of the right-of-way via South Framingham. Eventually Framingham proper became isolated as all commerce moved two miles south to the new rail station.

> **From the *Boston Advertiser* April 8, 1834**
>
> Boston & Worcester Rail Road—A locomotive ran yesterday on the railroad for the first time, as far as Davis's Tavern in Newton, a distance of eight or nine miles, accompanied by a party of the Directors and fifty or sixty other persons, for the purpose of making a trial of the engine, and an examination of the road. The party stopped several times for various purposes on the way out. They returned in 39 minutes including a stop of about six minutes for the purpose of attaching five cars loaded with earth. The engine travelled with ease at the rate of twenty miles an hour.

As construction continued through 1834, the railroad was opened to Needham (today's Wellesley) in July, to Ashland in September, and to Westboro in November. The first special train to operate to Worcester ran July 3, 1835; the next day a major celebration with fireworks officially marked the completion of the Boston & Worcester.

Passenger patronage was excellent from the first; freight revenues developed more slowly as shippers discovered rail's advantages. Double-tracking was undertaken in 1843. Five branch lines were opened between 1837 and 1848: Millbury Junction to Millbury in 1837 (p. 126); Natick to Saxonville in 1846 (p. 111); Riverside to Newton Lower Falls in 1847 (p. 108); Brookline Junction to Brookline Village in 1848 (p. 98); and South Framingham to Milford in 1848 (p. 112). Keenly feeling its isolation, Framingham agitated for service. A horse-powered branch was opened from the main line in 1849. Supplementing this branch six years later, the B&W leased the Agricultural Branch Railroad from Framingham to Marlboro in 1855, rails which were eventually continued to Fitchburg.

> **Boston & Worcester Wood-burning Locomotives in 1861**
>
> | Name | Weight (tons) | Builder | Service | Miles run to one cord of wood |
> |---|---|---|---|---|
> | Despatch | 28 | Bost. & Worc. | Passenger | 31 |
> | Elephant | 24 | " | " | 41.7 |
> | Bee | 22 | Wilmarth | " | 60.5 |
> | Falcon | 22 | " | " | 44.2 |
> | Fury | 22 | " | " | 43.2 |
> | William Penn | 22 | Hinkley | " | 37.4 |
> | Yankee* | 22 | " | " | 46 |
> | Comet | 19 | " | " | 41 |
> | Neptune | 19 | " | " | 53.1 |
> | Jupiter | 19 | " | " | 59.4 |
> | Brookline | 12 | Bury (England) | " | 46 |
> | Vesuvius | 25 | Bost. & Worc. | Freight | 37.7 |
> | Aetna | 25 | Wilmarth | " | 26.7 |
> | Niagara | 25 | " | " | 31 |
> | Panther | 22 | Hinkley | " | 36 |
>
> *Yankee was the first locomotive built in New England. It was completed at the Mill Dam Foundry in Roxbury in June 1834, and was modeled after an English engine imported for the Boston & Lowell.
>
> Source: Warren Jacobs

The Western Railroad

As we noted, the original purpose in chartering the Boston & Worcester was eventually to reach the Erie Canal, but the Legislature granted a charter only as far as Worcester. Building a railroad was a completely new venture for American entrepreneurs, and going first to Worcester was a way of making a manageable start on a huge project. Nonetheless the directors of the B&W incorporated individually as the Western Railroad on March 15, 1833, to build a line from Worcester through Springfield to the New York state line. It had authority to connect with any railroad built from Berkshire County to the Hudson River. A major boost came in 1834 from the New York Legislature when it chartered the Castleton & West Stockbridge (Castleton is nine miles south of Albany). Another line materialized a year later when the Hudson & Berkshire was chartered to build from Hudson, New York (20 miles south of Castleton) to the state line. The latter began grading work before Castleton

& West Stockbridge was started. It was poorly built with strap-iron-on-wood rail and was used only briefly.

It took two years of aggressive stock-selling meetings in Boston, Springfield, Lee, Pittsfield, and Albany before sufficient funds were amassed. In December 1835 the new directors met for the first time and elected officers. Further delay resulted when some subscribers failed to pay and new buyers had to be found, and it wasn't until the winter of 1836-37 that construction was begun at Charlton, 13 miles west of Worcester. After the Panic of 1837, the Commonwealth of Massachusetts lent money to finance construction through the Berkshires. Following such struggles it was a great relief to the backers when construction to the Connecticut River was completed on October 1, 1839, two months ahead of the date mandated by incorporation.

The City of Albany provided extra help when money for the West Stockbridge-Albany link wasn't raised. The city subscribed the needed money and hired the Western Railroad to build the connecting link, then leased back the completed trackage to the railroad.

Building the Western through the Berkshires was a great engineering feat for its time. At the highest point it reached 1,459 feet above sea level, yet grades were held to only 1.67 percent. Deep rock cuts were especially difficult and had to be accomplished with the tools of the time: pick axes, shovels, and black powder. Mule carts hauled the men and tools from place to place. The right-of-way crossed dozens of rivers and streams, all requiring bridges. Notable among these were nine stone arch bridges of particular beauty, three of which are extant (only one, modified, remains in operation). An unused bridge at Middlefield is pictured on page 17.

First through Boston-to-Albany timetable
From the *Boston Advertiser*, December 21, 1841

Westbound (read down)	AM/PM		Eastbound (read up)	
7:00	**3:00**	Boston	7:00	12:00 Noon
12:15	ar. **8:15**	Springfield		lv. 6:15
	lv. 7:00	Springfield	**12:30**	ar. 6:30
3:45	9:45	Pittsfield	9:45	**3:45**
5:30	11:30	Chatham	8:15	**2:15**
6:30	**12:30**	Albany	7:00	**1:00**

A daily stage met the morning train at Springfield and took passengers to Hartford for the train to New Haven, boat to New York.

Trains operated from Worcester to State Line on October 4, 1841. By temporarily using the inferior Hudson & Berkshire, the Western was able to reach Albany. Major celebrations were held between December 27 and 30, one day each in Albany, Springfield, and Boston. The Hudson & Berkshire was supplanted (some of its right-of-way was actually incorporated) when the Albany & West Stockbridge (successor to the Castleton & West Stockbridge) completed its State Line Tunnel.

The considerable engineering success of the Western

The Defalcation of Addison Ware

The Western Railroad experienced a nasty frisson in April 1850, after its president, Addison Gilmore, became suspicious about the bookkeeping practices of his Cashier in Springfield, Addison Ware. Having served the four prior presidents with complete trust—since August 1839—Ware was thought to be fully honest and competent. President Gilmore first became suspicious when his accounting people informed him that there were large balances due from Springfield which were not forthcoming. Gilmore's earlier notations of Ware's negligence now fueled his suspicions. With Board approval, he confronted Ware in Springfield, who agreed to put his books in order. Three visits later, Ware had produced nothing. Finally Ware presented Gilmore a statement as he passed through Springfield by train enroute to New York City and a boat to Europe. Gilmore sent it to his Committee on Accounts who got Ware to admit that he was short as much as $9,000 in cash.

Astonishingly the Committee allowed Ware to put affairs in order by himself; their justification was that things were such a mess they were afraid that no one else could do it. When Gilmore returned from three months in Europe in July, Ware abandoned the uncompleted books.

In the January 1851 Annual Report the Committee described what they'd found:

> "His cash account did not appear to have been balanced for years, nor has any memorandum been found since showing the balance of cash on hand, since the first opening of the books; not a figure had been put into the ledger for more than eighteen months. Two sets of books were kept open for entries when one set only would have been better. The entries of cash and other transactions in the cash books, journals, etc., were not regularly and fully made; settlements that had been made with individuals, firms, and corporations were not all entered in the books, but kept on memorandums or neglected altogether. The accounts with the connecting railroads were at loose ends; no stated and definite settlements had been made with them; the large running accounts with the Worcester Railroad and with the Albany station had not been settled for years, and the agents at the various stations upon the Road had not been required to make prompt and stated settlements."

When the dust settled, it was found that Ware had misappropriated $68,355, a huge sum of money. Indeed it was 5% of the year's total income, and it wiped out a third of the Western's contingency fund. A chastised Board of Directors was more diligent in its vigilance thereafter.

was due to the skill of chief engineer George Washington Whistler (father of the famous artist, James McNeil Whistler) who, along with his brother-in-law, William Gibbs McNeil, laid out an efficient route through very difficult terrain. Except for a two-mile stretch which was re-engineered in 1912 to ease curvature and grades, his choice of route has proven remarkably well conceived.

With the main line completed, the Western sought to quell potential competition. It leased the unbuilt Pittsfield & North Adams, chartered in 1842, and agreed to build it as a protective move to forestall any rivals who might covet the Pittsfield & North Adams charter. Similar circumstances led the Western to buy its lessor, the Hudson & Berkshire, after the little line went bankrupt.

With the Boston & Worcester and Western in place and operating successfully, logic called for their combining. Indeed that had been the concept all along. But their

> ### How Boston Lost Out
>
> Because of the fast growth of the traffic between the Western Railroad and its connection at Albany—the New York Central & Hudson River Railroad—President Chapin dreamed of the Western controlling the Central. The stock price became sufficiently depressed during the Civil War that Chapin thought the job could be done for $9 million. Try as he might, he could not pursuade Boston investors that it was worth the risk. He knew he could raise the first $1 million in Springfield, but his efforts to attract Boston financing came to naught. After Commodore Vanderbilt made his move in 1867 and took control of the Central, it became a moot issue. Boston lost out, but Chapin joined the NYC board and became a close confidant to Vanderbilt.

eventual joining together as the Boston & Albany was stupidly delayed for 25 years because of a heated disagreement about dividing freight revenues on through merchandise. The Boston & Worcester considered local traffic more lucrative than what the through traffic would yield it (the Western was more than twice as long), and was largely responsible for postponing an amalgamation. Even after a joint committee of the two roads recommended in 1845 that a union would be beneficial, the B&W stockholders stood firm.

Boston & Albany Railroad

Public opinion grew in favor of combining the two roads. With the coming of the Civil War, the public's attention was focused on the need for the railroads to support the Union cause. There was growing impatience with obstacles to joining the B&W and the Western. When the B&W's 30-year monopoly expired in 1863, the Western aired its plans to build a parallel line from Worcester to Boston. Again committees met to consider the consolidation. Again the B&W backed away as its stockholders defeated the proposal. In a forceful move, the Western petitioned the Massachusetts Legislature to build to Boston. The General Court authorized this in May 1867, unless the two roads were to join within four months. In the face of complete ruin, the B&W capitulated and the Boston & Albany Railroad was created on September 4, 1867. The Western's president, Chester W. Chapin, became president of the new railroad.

One of Chapin's first moves was to expedite the operation of the Grand Junction Railroad (page 66), giving the B&A a hugely profitable access to Boston's port traffic.

> ### Drawing Room Cars • Boston & Albany
> #### From the *Boston Advertiser*, Saturday, June 19, 1869
>
> *After Tuesday, June 15, 1869.* The Boston & Albany have just placed upon their line six New and Elegant Cars of the pattern known as Drawing Room Cars which for comfort and elegance of finish are unsurpassed. For ladies, families, and invalids they will be found particularly welcome and desirable. The above cars will run daily as follows from the Depot corner of Beach and Albany Streets, Boston for Springfield, Pittsfield, and Albany at 8:30 a.m. For Hartford, New Haven, and New York via Springfield at 8:00 a.m. and 3:00 p.m. Seats only 75 cents or $1.00 according to distance.
>
> C. O. Russell, Supt.
> Springfield

Important land acquisitions were made by the B&A in the 1870s which would prove essential for yard and engine facilities in the years to come. These included land parcels near the old Boston & Worcester depot at Beach Street, and in Back Bay, Allston, Brighton, Springfield, Worcester, and Rensselaer.

A new railroad in the 1870s called the Massachusetts Central was a cause for concern at the B&A. Proposed to run midway between the Fitchburg Railroad and the B&A, the Massachusetts Central was to be built via the Ware River Valley to Amherst and to the Hoosac Tunnel, then under construction. The Massachusetts Central had Legislative authority to buy the small Ware River Railroad, a purchase which would have threatened B&A territory. After several dubious financial maneuvers, President Chapin leased the Ware River for the B&A in 1873 (see the Ware River Branch section in Volume II).

The success of the Boston to Albany route aroused the ire of towns in the northern half of Massachusetts who were not served. A successful businessman from Fitchburg named Alvah Crocker took up the cause of

> ### First train from Atlantic to Pacific
> #### From the *Boston Advertiser* Saturday, May 21, 1870
>
> Grand Excursion, Boston Board of Trade, Boston to California, First Through Train from the Atlantic to the Pacific. Train consists of baggage car, smoking car, Pullman Cars *St. Cloud, Palmyra, Arlington, St. Charles, Marquette,* and *Revere.* The train will leave the crossing near where the [Peace Jubilee] Coliseum stood on Monday as near 9 o'clock as possible.
>
> #### From the *Boston Advertiser* Tuesday, May 24, 1870
>
> The palace cars of the Board of Trade Excursion party pulled away yesterday morning punctually at 9:30. A very large crowd of people were assembled to see the start and the cars were thronged until shortly before leaving time. The cars were beautifully decorated with flowers. The two engines that drew the train to Worcester, the *William Penn* and the *Meteor*, were both decorated with bunting and flowers. His Excellency Gov. Claflin was present and officials of the Boston & Albany accompanied the train. About two minutes before the start the Conductor shouted "All Aboard for California," and soon the magnificent train was in motion. The train arrived at Worcester at 10:26 a little ahead of time. A large crowd was present at the Western R. R. depot. The locomotives *Essex* and *Colorado* took the train from there.

building a through route to Albany on the north. The result was the eventual formation of three railroads: the Fitchburg, the Vermont & Massachusetts, and the Troy & Greenfield. The last included a provision for the Hoosac Tunnel, a gigantic construction project that took 24 years to complete, cost $17 million, and killed 196 men. When the Commonwealth finally sold the tunnel in 1887 to the Fitchburg Railroad for a mere $6 million, it rid itself of the annual interest on Hoosac's bonded debt, the largest single item in the state budget! Contrast this with the situation two decades earlier when Massachusetts came up with $2 million toward the construction of the Boston & Worcester. What happened in the interim was that railroads were sufficiently profitable to convince legislatures that governmental capital support was often in the public interest.

With the fast growth of industrial New England, there was plenty of business to divide among the two east-west routes in Massachusetts over the following decades. The Massachusetts Central failed to raise sufficient capital to complete its planned route and thus was never a threat. After ten years of operation the B&A was flourishing. The road had sufficient resources to improve its equipment and physical plant, including the replacing of all wooden bridges with iron. Most important, it was paying its stockholders a decent return.

In 1880 the B&A purchased the Springfield & Northeastern Railroad, a 48-mile line between Springfield and Athol which began operation in 1873. It was the B&A's last protective acquisition, and its purchase prevented either the Massachusetts Central or Fitchburg Railroads from using it for entry to Springfield. It became the B&A's Athol Branch (see Volume II) and, in an odd twist of fate, it was the first B&A branch to close, which it did in 1936 as part of the creation of the Quabbin Reservoir.

During 1879 and 1880 the B&A had its eyes on a possible takeover of the lucrative Boston & Providence Railroad. Discussions began innocently enough over finding a way to reroute B&A passenger trains out of the

This series of photos has been reproduced directly from a print of the Budd Company's film, CLEAR IRON, *which promoted its Rail Diesel Cars.* **First,** *from the top, the crossing gate attendant cranks down the gates after hearing a series of approach bells in his shanty. Busy crossings such as this one at the depot in Framingham required someone to be on duty 24 hours a day.* **Second,** *we are in the vestibule of a Budd Rail Diesel Car, called Beeliners on the New York Central, looking out at the traffic holding for our passing train.* **Third,** *the train is seen broadside as it passes the crossing shanty.* **Fourth,** *we are in the cab with the engineer as the train enters the station, where two ladies are talking on the platform.* **Fifth,** *we have a view of the stationary train in Framingham depot as several disembarking passengers come toward us. Clearly the fiming was done on several passes through the station, possibly not on scheduled trains. Notice that the engineer's view in the fourth frame is of the main depot, from the inbound track, while the train in the fifth frame is on the outbound track. A fascinating film record of a bygone era which is startling for its resolution considering that it came from motion picture film. RWJ collection.*

Basic Boston & Albany

unwieldy access to its Beach Street station (all trains had to cross Kneeland Street at grade), to move them into the commodious new B&P station in Park Square. After initial discussions revealed that joint operation of the depot would be impractical, the talks turned to combining the two railroads. After some roadblocks, a hasty proposal was made to the Legislature for a share-for-share consolidation. As advantages to the B&P, it was argued that it would get its own connection to the Union Freight Railroad, permit the use of the Grand Junction Branch in accessing railroads north of Boston, and eliminate the dangerous and time-wasting grade crossing of the two railroads at Dartmouth Street.

But perceptive critics saw in the B&A's rosy predictions a desire to control both the B&P's shore line and the boat connections to New York City (the Thames River at New London would not be bridged until 1892), so the project was defeated. Thus did the B&A build a new station at Kneeland Street in 1881. Also that year the B&A surveyed a possible line south from Springfield to New York City, and subsequently tried to buy the New Haven & Northampton Railroad, or some other existing line heading to New York. Ultimately the B&A settled on simply cooperating with the New Haven at Springfield and emphasizing its strengths as an east-west carrier.

> **BOSTON STATIONS OF THE B&W AND B&A**
>
> 1. WASHINGTON STREET, corner of present-day Marginal Road, April 16, 1834 to November 7, 1836. First railroad station in Boston.
> 2. BEACH STREET, corner of Lincoln and Albany Streets, November 7, 1836 to September 5, 1881.
> 3. KNEELAND STREET, opposite Lincoln Street, September 5, 1881 to July 23, 1899.
> 4. SOUTH STATION, July 23, 1899 to present.

The main line between Boston and Riverside was expanded from double track to three and (mostly) four tracks in 1882, greatly expanding the capacity and flexibility of the trackage. All stations except Trinity Place were built on the south side of the right-of-way, with the southern two tracks serving local trains. Main line trains were handled by the two northern tracks. Telegraph and telephone lines along the B&A main line were all located on the north side of the tracks for its entire length.

The Highland Branch (page 98) was established as an important commuter route in 1886 after the B&A exercised its right (negotiated in the late 1860s) to buy part of the Boston, Hartford & Erie. The B&A only wanted the six-mile section from Boston to Cook Street, from where it built an additional three miles of track northwest to Riverside. This so-called "circuit" layout enabled trains from Boston to travel via the branch as far as Riverside, then return via the main line without turning the engine, and vice versa. The Highland Branch became home of the B&A's famous Tank Engines beginning in 1906 (page 35).

These double-ended locomotives, some of which were the heaviest and most powerful of their type in the world, were perfectly suited to the branch's steep grades and sharp curves, and to the increasing size and weight of commuter trains.

In 1884 the B&A purchased the newly built Webster Branch (see Volume II), where it quickly derived important revenue from servicing the Slater Woolen Co.

Beginning in 1883 the railroad embarked upon an ambitious program to build modern stone stations on its route. Henry Hobson Richardson, designer of Boston's landmark Trinity Church, was the chosen architect. He completed nine designs before his death in 1886, then 23 more designs were produced by his successor firm, Shepley, Rutan and Coolidge. Subsequently the B&A retained other architects to produce several more stations in similar styles. Together as a body of design, these stations did more than anything else to define the railroad's visual appearance for six decades ("Magnificent Stations" in Volume II provides more detail).

Passenger operations in Boston were improved dramatically with the opening of South Station. New Haven Railroad trains started using the new depot first on January 1, 1899, with B&A's trains transferring there from the Kneeland Street station seven months later on July 23. The station was operated by The Boston Terminal Co., which was owned by both the New Haven and the B&A in a 70/30 split (see Chapter II).

By 1880 the B&A was interchanging large amounts of east-west traffic with the NYC, deriving some two-thirds of its freight revenue from the connection. The two roads signed a formal compact March 3, 1880 which essentially treated interchange traffic as if it were running on a single railroad, though property and earnings were kept separate. The agreement was written initially for five years but stayed in effect until the B&A was leased in 1900.

By 1899 the NYC made it known that it wanted direct control of the B&A, largely for access and profits at the port of Boston. The current B&A president, William Bliss, realized that were the B&A to resist, the NYC could probably acquire the Fitchburg Railroad with its Hoosac Tunnel route for access across Massachusetts. After some stockholder skirmishing, a mutual agreement was hammered out, the Legislature gave its stamp, and the B&A by lease officially became part of the New York Central Lines on September 26, 1900.

New York Central Takes Over

In a move which would prejudice the success of its takeover, the New York Central failed to judge New England sensitivities as it replaced the B&A name on locomotives rolling stock with its own. Chauvinistic New Englanders were not pleased. To its credit, the NYC brought new and larger locomotives to the B&A, increased the number of through trains, improved the food service onboard the diners and club cars, and planned a third track in sections of the Berkshires to move trains more efficiently.

Severe winters during the first years of the lease caused many operational difficulties. Edgar Van Etten was the new manager brought in from the NYC and, had he been more sensitive to the public relations needs of handling the intricacies of the lease, might have lessened tensions. By 1907 public opinion against the NYC was fueled by opportunistic politicians and the ever-alert press, and the Legislature and the Massachusetts Railroad Commission both launched investigations. Van Etten stupidly opined that Boston's best days as a grain export center were in the past, casting himself in an especially unsympathetic light.

The Railroad Commission laid down some strict performance standards that September, requiring that passenger service records be filed periodically (in fairness it must be noted that other New England railroads had suffered equally from weather-induced problems). Also, the NYC was to provide details of all B&A expenditures as well as all plans for improvements. Six senior NYC officials came to Boston for a round of meetings just two days following the Commission's report. Van Etten was out. Alfred H. Smith, general superintendent of the NYC, was appointed vice president and general manager of the B&A, with offices in New York. J. H. Hustis would be general manager with offices in Boston. Perhaps the most significant change to come from the shake-up was that thereafter the two railroads were operated as a single entity rather than two.

Hustis' charm and diplomatic skills endeared him to many, and he capably steered the organization through its difficulties. The B&A name was returned to all equipment, and NYC management let its Boston people run the show, assuaging public opinion. Hustis went to the New Haven Railroad in 1913 and later to the Boston & Maine.

To increase through passenger service from Boston to the west, the NYC introduced Boston sections of several of its popular named trains. These included the *Chicago Special*, *Southwestern Limited*, *Wolverine*, and *Western Express*. Most famous of all was the *Twentieth Century Limited* which was introduced between New York and Chicago on June 15, 1902; the Boston section first ran October 3, 1909. The switching logistics at Albany were always troublesome for such a fast-carded limited (and remain so for Amtrak). The NYC inaugurated streamlined equipment on the *Twentieth Century* June 15, 1938, shortening the schedule to compete with the Pennsylvania Railroad's *Broadway Limited*, and making impractical the inclusion of the older heavyweight cars of the Boston section. The same day the NYC introduced the *New England States*, a through train between Boston and Chicago with sleeping, dining, and club cars (later adding coaches) which would last nearly three decades.

The B&A's autonomy was left intact until about 1950, when difficulties arose from a string of six general managers in five and a half years. To improve relations, the resident vice president position was revived in 1954. New England had largely outgrown its insular chauvinism with the growth of national companies during the first half of the century, so when the NYC put its own name back on the rolling stock, there was virtually no protest. The NYC was obliged to pay all B&A taxes as part of its lease. The only extant taxes in 1900 were property taxes, but later corporate income taxes were levied by the Federal government, and other taxes accrued as well. By the early 1950s this burden had become alarmingly large and the NYC sought ways to ameliorate such costs. In December 1954 the NYC petitioned the Interstate Commerce Commission to acquire control of the B&A by purchasing its stock. Several transactions were required to accomplish the desired merger, which finally became effective April 3, 1961, when the Boston & Albany officially became part of the New York Central.

The NYC was itself combined into the Penn Central on February 1, 1968, in a long contemplated merger with the Pennsylvania Railroad. The new corporation went down in flames just 28 months later on June 21, 1970 in one of the most famous and nasty bankruptcies in American business history (the largest to date). Operation was continued tenuously under receivership with the aid of guaranteed federal loans until April 1, 1976 when the Consolidated Rail Corporation—Conrail, created by Congress from seven bankrupt Northeast railroads, took over. Among the systems acquired by Conrail were the remnants of the former Boston & Albany, including the last of its commuter trains to Framingham. Barely a year later, in March 1977, their operation was assumed by the Boston & Maine (under contract to the MBTA).

Although Conrail initially cost American taxpayers $7 billion, it was in the black by 1983. The company was sold through a public stock offering in March 1987 for $1.88 billion (employees retained some 15% of the stock). It has performed well and remained profitable ever since. A bitter dispute arose in mid-1996 between CSX Corporation and Norfolk Southern over which railroad would prevail in its enduring quest to purchase Conrail. No resolution had been announced by press time, though it was widely speculated that the Conrail properties would be split between the two railroads. One important goal was to reopen northeastern cities to direct rail competition.

The Boston & Albany, one of America's early successful railroads, will no doubt continue in helping New England to prosper after a century and a half of operation.

In American railroading, baggage tags were made of brass for the first six decades, beginning about 1841. This one from the Boston & Worcester is an early example from maker John Robbins, a prominent supplier. Michael J. Sullivan collection/Brian Solomon photo.

WOODEN CARS AND IRON MEN
LEWIS H. BULLARD, 1941

Many readers are familiar with the modern motive power and efficient operation of the Boston & Albany, but probably there are only a few who recollect the power which was considered most capable in the last part of the nineteenth century, and the operation of the road at that time.

As a boy, from about 1886 to 1900, I lived in the town of Wellesley, most of that time directly across the street from the Wellesley Hills depot. When my family first moved to Wellesley, the Boston & Albany had four tracks as far as Riverside only. The main line from Riverside to Wellesley Hills had many curves, and a steep grade (for those days) in the vicinity of what is now Wellesley Farms. The latter station was then called Rice's Crossing, a flag stop with an old wooden shanty; there was a hobo jungle adjacent to the steep grade, convenient for the "Knights of the Road" to hop freights. The Wellesley Hills station was a long wooden affair, with the freight house connected and the village post office at one end. This station was first known as "Grantville" [originally Needham, it became Grantville when the Charles River RR opened to Needham]. There was one side-track at the Hills, serving the freight house, and a ramp platform for unloading horses and cattle; also a cross-over between the main tracks. At Wellesley there were two sidings for freight trains to back into, a few stub tracks, a cross-over, and a brick pumping-plant; freight engines would take water there.

To illustrate the fact that local passenger traffic was quite heavy in the middle eighties, that travel to New York City exceeded that to the Middle West before the Shore Line was fully developed, and that the Northern Division of the Old Colony was an important feeder, I am giving from memory the approximate detailed west-bound schedule of trains out of Boston (omitting local trains to Riverside). This will also show to Railfandom that it required real operating brains to sandwich in the freights and work trains, with light power and without modern safety devices. I can vouch for the fact that before the advent of trolley-cars and automobiles, all B&A trains were well patronized.

5:00 a.m.	Albany local (advertised to stop at any station for passengers for Palmer and west, provided notice was received before 9:00 the previous evening!)
6:30 a.m.	South Framingham local (now Framingham).
7:00 a.m.	Springfield local (express to South Framingham, with the three rear cars for Marlboro and Fitchburg via the Old Colony).
7:45 a.m.	South Framingham local.
8:30 a.m.	*Albany Day Express* (Wagner Parlor Car to Albany, and two mail cars for New York City).
9:00 a.m.	*New York Express* (All NYNH&H cars; dinner at Springfield).
9:30 a.m.	Saxonville local.
10:20 a.m.	South Framingham local.
11:00 a.m.	*New York Express* (All NYNH&H cars; connecting train from Springfield to Albany).
11:45 a.m.	Worcester local with cars for Marlboro and Fitchburg.
1:00 p.m.	Worcester local.
2:00 p.m.	Milford, also Marlboro and Fitchburg.
2:30 p.m.	Worcester-Springfield local (passed at Worcester by the 3:00 p.m. train).
3:00 p.m.	*Western Express* (Wagner Palace sleeping cars; supper at Springfield).
3:45 p.m.	South Framingham local.
4:00 p.m.	*New York Express* (this was the crack train of the day, with all B&A cars, and was the only train carrying a diner at that time.)
4:15 p.m.	*Worcester Express*, with cars for Milford, also Marlboro, and Fitchburg (there were about ten cars on this train).
4:50 p.m.	Milford local
5:00 p.m.	Springfield
5:25 p.m.	Worcester local, with cars for Marlboro and Fitchburg.
5:50 p.m.	Saxonville
6:20 p.m.	South Framingham local
7:15 p.m.	*Western Express* (Wagner sleepers).
7:45 p.m.	Mail and express cars for the west; no coaches.
9:00 p.m.	South Framingham local.
10:30 p.m.	Mail and express, with a sleeper for Albany; no coaches).
11:00 p.m.	*New York Night Express* (connection to Albany).
11:15 p.m.	South Framingham local.

Wagner Palace Cars were used on all western trains, and Wagner Parlor Cars on Albany trains. On the New York trains the B&A and the NYNH&H used their own cars; for the 11:00 p.m. train the B&A furnished its own sleepers on alternate nights. Cars on the Marlboro-Fitchburg trains were divided about evenly between the B&A and the Old Colony. Local trains were equipped with Miller couplers but the through trains had Janney couplers. Steam heat was used, and all cars had open platforms. The newest cars were lighted with Pintsch gas; the older ones had kerosene lamps.

A local freight for South Framingham left Boston early in the morning. A milk train left around noon, with quite a string of cars for the Old Colony. A Worcester freight, with cars of the various local companies, left in the early afternoon. The through freights were sandwiched in between passenger trains or ran at night, engines and crews going as far as Worcester only.

Newton Lower Falls station is within the boundaries of the town of Wellesley. Two locomotives were housed at night at Lower Falls. One made a trip to Boston and back; the other ran a two-car connection to Riverside, and on at least one trip a day was a mixed train. On one or two other trips a coach or two was handled through to Boston on a Circuit train [see page 98].

The Saxonville train crew made two round trips to Boston and ran a mixed job to Natick in the middle of the day.

Two passenger engines were used on the Milford branch, each making one round trip to Boston. Besides the local passenger engines, a freight engine for the Milford branch and an 0-4-0 switcher were housed at South Framingham.

B&A 4-4-0 American No. 220 is an example of the type Lewis Bullard saw with brass numbers under the cab window. This photograph was taken at Charlton depot in 1892, the same year this C-31d-class locomotive was built at Rhode Island. In 1893 it was renumbered as B&A No. 150, and again in 1900 as New York Central & Hudson River No. 752. Bob's Photo/Brian R. Scace collection.

Now for the motive power. All names had been removed from the engines, and all were painted simply in black, with brass number plates on the front of the boiler and on each side of the cab; numbers were also painted on the rear of the tender. No road designation was lettered on either engine or tender. Most of the passenger engines had been fitted with extended front ends and capped straight stacks. It is needless to say that all were of the American (4-4-0) type. All passenger engines had been fitted with air-brake pumps and brake trainline, but bell-cord was still in use for signal purposes. The locomotives in local service were straight-boiler affairs and probably none weighed over 40 tons, the majority being much lighter. The engines on through trains had wagon-top boilers and were of standard 45-ton weight. The lighter engines generally had 16 x 22 cylinders, and the drivers were from 60 in. to 66 in.; the larger engines had 18 x 22 cylinders.

Freights between Boston and Worcester were all hauled by American-type engines, but with larger cylinders and smaller drivers. Most of the freight engines had straight boilers, but a few of the newer engines had wagon tops. No. 180, handling the milk train, was the only Mogul on the east end of the road. The switchers were of the 0-4-0 type, with 16 x 24 cylinders and 48 in. drivers. All of the freight engines carried diamond stacks, and with about two exceptions the switchers were diamond-stacked.

About 1890 a large order of new freight engines of the 4-4-0 type was received from Rhode Island. These engines were diamond-stacked and had 20 x 26 cylinders and 54 in. drivers. In 1893 the first really big engines (for those days) arrived on the east end of the line. These were two Ten-Wheelers (Nos. 11 and 12) and four Eight-Wheelers, all from Rhode Island and for use in passenger service. The Eight-Wheelers did not work too well, at least at first, and they were often assigned to locals. I remember one occasion when a diamond-stacked freight engine had to haul one of these engines *and its train* into Boston.

About 1895 the B&A received its first big Eight-Wheelers from Schenectady, and soon thereafter some of the Consolidations began showing up on freights into Boston.

In the first part of this article, mention was made that the line from Riverside through the Wellesleys had only two tracks, many curves, and a stiff grade. Soon after my arrival in town the road started work eliminating curves and four-tracking, first to Lake Crossing [midway between Wellesley and Natick] and later to South Framingham. During the progress of this work I was in my glory; having just recovered from scarlet fever and measles, and being kept out of school, I was able to be on hand to oversee the whole job. A kind engineer invited me to ride on the 163, one of the engines assigned to gravel service. From then on I was either in an engine cab or on a work car until the job was completed. Two or three steam shovels were employed, and many ledges had to be drilled and blasted. Four-wheeled gravel cars were used on the first part of the work, and a large gang of men was on hand to dump the cars and spread the gravel.

Engines 114, 141, 163, 174, 194, and 60 were among those used when the work first started. No. 194, the old "Westboro," renumbered 276, ended her days on the Lower Falls branch. No. 174 was the regular work-train engine and hauled a little old passenger car with longitudinal seats and a strong smell of garlic; the train crews called this "The Stinker." No. 60 was a Hinkley-built switcher, named "Pusher." As the work progressed toward Wellesley and Natick, flat cars were used for gravel, with a scraper device for unloading; several locomotives from the western end of the road were put on the job, and among them were an Eddy engine and two Rhode Island moguls.

The Saxonville train was hauled by No. 205, the "Saxonville," built by the B&A in 1872. George Reid was conductor, and the road gave him time off when he was elected to the Legislature. Perly Ordway was brakeman, a man of strong religious temperament who sang the names of the stations. The baggage-master was a small man who wouldn't allow cigarette smoking in the baggage end of the combination car.

These engines ran east of Worcester only occasionally. In times of heavy travel, for double-heading in snowstorms and as spares, a few of them were sometimes seen at the Boston end of the line.

Long excursion trains from Springfield, Worcester, and other points were frequently run in the summer season, and some of the Eddys or other west-end power would generally haul them. On the arrival of steamers from Europe there were immigrant specials to the West, starting from East Boston. These cars were attached to the 7:15 p.m. express, or sometimes run as a second section.

The first freight engines, I remember, had brakes on the drivers only. The freight cars had link-and-pin couplers, and break-in-twos were frequent. The cabooses were mostly four-wheeled, except for some side-door affairs used on local freights to carry merchandise. The brakemen rode on the tops of the cars, with strong clubs in their hands. In times of heavy snowfall the old wedge plows went through with two or more engines, and trains were

On a rainy day circa 1896, a team of photographers is positioned along the four-track main line at Riverside. The focus of their attention is brand-new No. 211, a 4-4-0 Class C-37 American type locomotive, recently delivered from Schenectady. It was renumbered B&A No. 1151 in 1900, and NYC No. 242 in 1912. The train is stationary for the photo session. Note the truss rods on the wooden, round-topped cars. Paul T. Carver collection.

An oldish conductor (I believe named Rice) handled the Lower Falls train. As business fell off, he and the engineer (no fireman) handled the one-car train with old 276.

No. 164, built by the B&A, and named "William Bliss" for the president of the road, hauled the morning train from Milford to Boston, returning at 2:00 p.m. and making another round trip as far south as South Framingham. No. 139, "Union," built by William Mason in 1885, did the balance of passenger work on the Milford branch.

Nos. 122, 124, and 116 were early engines on the 6:30 South Framingham local. No. 116, built in 1880, retained her diamond stack to the last, was renumbered 221 and ended up in freight service as 101. The combination baggage-car and smoker on this train was No. 1.

The Pay Car was a one-car special in the old days. It was quite often hauled by one of the famous Eddy engines with two straight pipes for steam domes and a square sand box.

double-headed and reduced in length.

Along with improvement in power the passenger equipment also began to improve in the nineties. Sleeping cars were equipped with narrow vestibules, and the B&A bought about three complete trains of narrow-vestibuled coaches. The last word in equipment were two complete wide-vestibuled trains for the 4:00 p.m. New York Express. Of course, before 1900 several new western trains had been added, and I believe Pullmans had replaced Wagner cars. By this time patent couplers were becoming universal and air-brakes had been applied to freight cars; however, it was some time before steel equipment appeared, and trailing wheels were applied to locomotives, and of course air-conditioning had not been dreamed of.

We have a lot to see on the railroads in these modern times, but there was a lot of romance in the good old days of Wooden Cars and Iron Men.

MEMORIES OF THE BOSTON & ALBANY
STANLEY H. SMITH, circa 1950

My first sight of a steam train back in 1898 was in Newton Centre when I saw a Diamond-Stack Eight-Wheeler pulling a gravel train, smoke and dust flying like nobody's business. I was six years old. With that I became inoculated with "railroad fever" forever. The fever has subsided with the changeover to diesels, which are about as fascinating as a trailer truck.

In 1900 my family moved to Auburndale on the four-track line of the B&A. I lived there four years and I guess I spent two of the four sitting on the railroad fence watching the trains go by. There were plenty of them. Once I saw four trains passing each other at the same point. When I first moved there the equipment was painted Boston & Albany, but when I left four years later it was New York Central System. The Circuit trains were hauled by small Eight-Wheelers at the turn of the century. Occasionally I'd see two Ten-Wheelers, B&A Nos. 220 and 221, later relettered NYCS Nos. 2030 and 2031, although these two seldom came to Boston, being mostly used west of Springfield.

The freight engines were of two types, small Eight-Wheelers and small Consolidations with drivers about four feet in diameter. Most of the small eight-wheel passenger engines were used on the Circuit locals.

The engine pulling the passenger cars on the Newton Lower Falls line was a Diamond-Stacker. At that time the Falls Branch trains passed west of Riverside on mainline track 4, crossed the Charles River, then left the main line to go through the Riverside recreation grounds to Newton Lower Falls [see page 108].

The biggest thrill of my railroad watching was in 1902 when a freight came down the line from Worcester pulled by a Consolidation. Looming high behind came a new Atlantic. This engine was soon a common sight on the B&A expresses, along with five more like it. When these engines first arrived, small wooden cabins were built over their pilots, housing M.I.T. students who checked tractive effort and efficiencies.

Lest I forget, the switches at Riverside—in the engine and car yard—were stub type. Every morning, cars for the Auburndale siding were brought down by a Diamond-Stacker, the engine running backward. The train, with no caboose, ran on track 4 over to track 1 against westbound traffic. This was because the switch into the Auburndale siding was from track 1. The siding ran almost to the Commonwealth Avenue Bridge, and then split into a track leading to the freight house.

In addition to the engines described above, there was also the president's car built on top of a small Eight-Wheeler, named *Berkshire* (No. 31), with an upright boiler. The smoke pipe ran through the middle with a bench, like a table, upon which was an elaborate silver set. There were three wicker chairs on each side of the table. It had plate-glass windows and was entered on both sides by elaborate steps over the cylinders. One day I saw it on a sidetrack at Riverside and crept over to it. No one was in it so I climbed aboard and had a good look around. Spotting someone coming, I climbed down and ran like Hell. Years later, after I retired, I met a former B&A vice president who told me the New York Central and the Delaware & Hudson had several similar vehicles, and that during summer weekends these vice presidents would all meet in the Adirondacks and have a ball for themselves.

Stanley H. Smith spent the four years between age 8 and 12 living in Auburndale, where he constantly watched trains. Later he would work here as a baggage man in this depot, the first of nine B&A stations designed by the renowned Henry Hobson Richardson, completed in 1881 at a cost of $16,290. It featured landscaping by Frederick Law Olmstead which, as can been seen in this 1910 postcard, was very lush indeed. It must have been a special experience to board a train from such a wonderfully maintained station. Richard B. Sanborn collection.

Basic Boston & Albany

Stanley H. Smith first saw this Schenectady Compound when it was B&A No. 220. It was renumbered NYC No. 2030 in 1900 and B&A No. 702 in 1912. Smith observed its only mate, NYC No. 2031, pulling the milk train. The engine's two cylinders were of different dimensions; the left one measured 22 in., while the right one measured 34 in. Employees called them "Slam-Bangs." Robert A. Buck collection.

In 1904—when I was 12—I had a pal my age whose father, Charles Temple, was a conductor running passenger trains around the Circuit, from Boston via Brookline to Riverside and returning via the main line. He often took us for Sunday afternoon rides, starting at Auburndale, going to Boston, treating us to ice cream at a Dewey Square restaurant, and then back to Auburndale. The cars had open-platforms and windows in the ends. We would sit on the car's front seat. As the tenders were small, we could watch the signals and, best of all, the engineer and fireman—we did this many times.

Outside the South Station there was a turntable where the Circuit engines were turned, a good watching spot. We also watched the two switch engines used to shift the cars at the station's yard. There were both 0-4-0s with slanted tenders—one a New Haven, the other a B&A engine. One night a Circuit engine bound for Brookline split the switch at Brookline Junction and tipped onto its side, killing the engineer. After the NYC took over, all the rolling stock was renamed and renumbered. For a time the service was so bad that Boston newspapers referred to the B&A as the "Boston & Almost."

When I was 16 in 1908 I heard about the B&A yard at Beacon Park, and from then on I traveled from Dedham to Allston by trolley on pleasant Saturdays, took engine pictures, developed and printed them during the week, and returned the following Saturday to sell copies to the engine crews. I

Stanley H. Smith remembers when the fast trains began to be pulled by New York Central 3500-series Pacifics. No. 3530 shows off its beautiful lines and proportions at South Station in 1909. She was built at Schenectady in September 1908, renumbered B&A No. 535 in 1912, and finally dismantled on October 5, 1935. Bob's Photo/Brian R. Scace collection.

Here is the other type of Ten-Wheeler which Smith describes as having appeared, the New York Central 1900-series. He called them beautiful engines which were used both in passenger and freight service. Kevin T. Farrell collection.

made my spending money at this for quite a while, and in so doing saw a lot of B&A motive power: one Diamond-Stack Eight-Wheeler (used as a switcher); one small old-time Consolidation (also a switcher); many Atlantics and Pacifics; one Mogul (the only one I ever saw on the Albany); a Mallet (1249); Ten-Wheelers (1900s); a couple of Mastadons, 4-8-0—all lettered for New York Central System [with a small "B&A"]. Directly in front of the Allston station there was a locomotive repair shop and often times a newly painted engine was in full view—what a thrill this was to us.

Double-enders started replacing many of the small circuit engines. The fast trains were now headed by Pacifics—4-6-2s numbered in the NYC 3500s. The Atlantics were still NYC 3900s, though some Atlantics numbered in the 2900 series were probably used mostly west of Springfield. Still another type of Ten-Wheeler had appeared: the NYC 1900s—beautiful engines—were used both in passenger and freight service. One of them pulled the fast freight called BN which left Boston every noon.

In 1912 I got a job as baggageman at the Auburndale Depot, where the stationmaster was a Mr. McClain, a fine fellow. It was a seven-day-a-week job for which I got $11.20. Not much money, but my profit was seeing the trains go by. There were lots of them: locals drawn by Double-enders; Pacifics pulling the fancy trains; Atlantics running the locals from Springfield to Boston; large Consolidations and Ten-Wheelers pulling the freights. These were now all being renumbered and relettered back to B&A. Old Ten-Wheeler No. 2031 [Schenectady Compound] would lead the milk train. Only one Eight-Wheeler was left; it ran on the job from Saxonville to Boston.

There was one novelty; a New Haven train [for Marlboro and Fitchburg] ran on track 1 from Boston to Framingham. It was pulled by a small Eight-Wheeler. The engine and cars were all from the New Haven.

In January 1913 the agent at Longwood (circuit route) took a long vacation. I took his place until he returned in May. It wasn't much of a place to see train variety, as nearly all passenger locals were drawn by Double-enders. A variation was the local freight, pulled by a large Consolidation, ambling its way to Riverside. I would never see it come back, and I often wondered what became of it [the eastbound local freight returned via the main line, ed.]. Also, a New Haven train from Newton Highlands and further south would fly by for Boston in mid-afternoon.

I quit the railroad when the regular agent came back in May 1913. I still watched the B&A, especially the Circuit trains. Now the Double-enders had taken over from those small eight-wheel Circuit engines, which were all gone by 1920.

The Last Two Decades Of B&A Steam

Brian R. Scace, 1992

The New York Central was famous for its smooth, virtually gradeless mainline between New York and Chicago. The slogans said it all. Every evening the "Great Steel Fleet" set sail over the "Water Level Route." When night fell and the diner emptied, the phrase "You Can Sleep" was once again tested and verified.

Subsidiary Boston & Albany was anything but typical of the NYC. It was a railroad replete with tight curves and steep grades, cleverly woven through the Berkshire Hills of Massachusetts to the Atlantic. Because of the difference in topography, the locomotives on the B&A differed markedly from their cousins on the rest of the system. Although there was a family resemblance, the different requirements in performance characteristics kept the B&A roster close to home. As the 1930s became the 1950s, however, war and technology would change all that.

Passenger traffic right before the World War II was handled by twenty J2 Hudsons and a supporting host of K-class Pacifics. The Hudsons were the newest road power on the roster, the last having been delivered in 1931. The Pacifics were all pre-WW I examples except for the K3 types transferred from the New York Central in 1938. These engines were erected in 1918 and eventually proved themselves to be the only successful 79 inch-drivered power on the B&A during our survey. More on this later.

Gone were the K6 heavy Pacifics to the Pittsburgh & Lake Erie, many of the early K-class engines, as well as the last of the Americans (C-class) and Ten Wheelers (F-class) by the end of the 1930s.

In freight service much the same situation existed. The famed Berkshires in class A1 were the backbone of the freight roster on the mainline. While the NYC cast its lot with Mohawks (L-class) from Alco, the B&A took delivery of a total of 55 A1 types with 63 inch drivers from Lima. These engines represented the newest road freight power on the line. The last ten A1c types were delivered in 1930.

Retained from myriad attempts to get freight over the Berkshire Hills were other 63 inch-drivered engines of the Mikado (H5-class) and Consolidation (G-class) designs. This driver size became the de facto standard freight driver on the road excepting Six Wheel and Eight Wheel (B- and U-class) switchers.

Gone from the freight roster by 1935 were the 4-8-0 Mastadons (scrapped), the H10 heavy Mikados (transferred to the Big Four), the Z-class USRA 2-10-2s (sold to the Canadan National), and the NE2 articulateds (scrapped).

The depression brought an austerity to American railroads and the B&A was not immune. There was no money to replace old equipment and precious little to maintain that on hand. The showcase power, the Hudsons and Berkshires, was already ten years old by the start of WW II. Most of the remaining roster dated back to WW I or before, and the picture was much the same with other types of rolling stock. Few freight or passenger cars were replaced between 1930 and 1940. This era saw very limited upgrading of the motive power fleet and rolling stock, not only on the B&A but across the nation. This would have a profound effect on railroading in the following decade.

With the outbreak of war in Europe and Asia, the already aging rosters of America's railroads, instead of being replaced as they came due, were expanded with newer types as fast as an awakening economy would allow. One example of the radical change in locomotive and rolling stock utilization can be seen in photos of old 35T truss-rod boxcars in through-service long after they were to be outlawed for interchange. Another example is quoted in Don Ball, Jr.'s *Decade of the Trains—the 1940s*, where in 1939 only 527 tons (about 18 cars) of oil passed over the B&A. By 1942 the coastal U-Boat threat mandated that 1,599,828 tons (the equivalent of three daily 42-car trains) be shipped over the line. These two examples illustrate vividly that old equipment could not be retired, but only supplemented with new stock.

With the war came radical changes in power utilization on both the B&A and NYC. The B&A's own roster became much less restricted to home rails, and what NYC power was suitable to the Berkshire Hills made appearances on the B&A. Berkshires ran regularly from Boston to Dewitt with oil trains while Mohawks appeared in West Springfield and Beacon Park.

Because of the dramatic rise in traffic, maximum locomotive utilization was imperative. Terminal functions and maintenance were reduced as far as the law would allow to increase each locomotive's availability. This had an adverse effect on the general condition of the roster, especially in a mountain environment.

Unfortunate timing played a role, too. In the year before Pearl Harbor, the NYC attempted to streamline its maintenance by moving the B&A's heavy locomotive maintenance off-line to NYC's West Albany Shops. Service and light repair continued at Selkirk, West Springfield, and Beacon Park.

These factors—equipment age, a massive swing in traffic, a mountain profile, and maintenance changes—all found the B&A's power in a critically exhausted state by war's end in 1945.

During the war two significant events occurred which would have a profound effect on both NYC and B&A motive power policy. One was a policy change between the Central and its subsidiary roads, and one was a change in locomotive technology. First let us examine the policy change.

Before the war the subsidiary roads were granted some autonomy in their operation within the System. Indeed the B&A behaved extremely independently compared to the other lines comprising the NYC family. This stemmed from the turn of the century when the NYC leased the B&A and began to re-letter its equipment. Proud Bostonians were so publicly angered by the new owner's audacious move that the NYC retreated, leaving the B&A with its name on the rolling stock and a fair measure of independence.

In January 1949, NYC L-3a 4-8-2 No. 3014 is departing Worcester Union Station with Train 22, the eastbound Lake Shore Limited. Within two years, all B&A operations would be dieselized. The roof of the old Union Station is visible in the background at right. Stephen R. Payne photo.

During WW II, however, a quite natural and economically sound development manifested itself. The first obvious sign of the change in relationship between the parent road and its subsidiaries was a subtle name change in the 1930s from New York Central *Lines* to New York Central *System*. Various changes were made in the System structure such as the previously mentioned locomotive maintenance shift off the B&A proper to West Albany, but generally such practices as lettering rolling stock for subsidiary roads and ordering specially designed locomotives for a particular line continued.

The NYC decided that such individualities in wartime were not economically sound or efficient, so when it went shopping for what power it could get, it considered the needs of the majority. Since the B&A was not operationally representative of the System as a whole, its specific needs were not foremost in mind during the procurement of the Mohawks (L3- and L4-class), or of the Niagaras (S-class). As it turned out, the Mohawks served on the B&A in various capacities, but the Niagaras—built 1945-46—for a variety of reasons did not.

The technology change went largely unheralded on the B&A. On October 25, 1944 the first road-freight-diesel-set passed through Pittsfield on the way to West Springfield led by FT No. 1600. The success of this trip was in its way as dramatic as the much more highly publicized trip of the first Berkshire in competition with an H10 over the road in 1925. In the FT's case, the time between Pittsfield and Washington Summit—the Hinsdale Grade—was trimmed by more than 10 minutes (with the usual helper assigned). It was thus found that an off-the-shelf diesel locomotive could perform the tasks required on the B&A, and the solution for the problem of specialized power for a profile unlike anywhere else on the System was found. The FT went into service the next day without fanfare.

In the immediate postwar years NYC management had several decisions to make with regard to the entire system which directly affected the B&A. The most obvious problem was that of replacing the pre-depression era rosters of locomotives and rolling stock. Right after the war the NYC rostered more than one thousand 36 ft. boxcars. By 1950 they were virtually gone. At the same time the largest order for passenger equipment in history was placed with Budd and Pullman Standard, decimating the heavyweight fleet.

Because of the advancing age of the Pacifics in passenger service, as well as a projected boom in postwar travel, there was an effort to upgrade passenger motive power. Though it is not documented, one could surmise that, given the success of

Basic Boston & Albany 33

NYC No. 5426 crosses Concord Street in Framingham eastbound on Sunday, February 2, 1947—Groundhog Day. This J3 Hudson, along with sister 5429, was streamlined for the 1941 edition of the Empire State Express which debuted on that infamous day, December 7. This is the only color photo we found of a streamlined Hudson on the B&A, though we have reports of sightings in 1943 and 1946, the latter also with a "PT" tender. We are grateful to George W. Turnbull for confirming the location: "I can match the small white building directly in front of the loco to one that still stands today. The signals protected the New Haven crossing on a diamond (current location of CP21). The white fence was removed a few years ago and a cement block garage was built." Stanley Smith photo/Norton D. Clark collection.

the K3 Pacifics with their 79 inch drivers that arrived on the B&A just prior to World War II, the next logical step in passenger power transfers would be like-drivered Hudsons. Thus in the late 1940s a number of J1 and J3 types in the Harmon-Albany pool drew assignments on B&A passenger work. The huge centipede "PT" tenders assigned to most J3 and some J1 Hudsons, however, were restricted from certain key parts of the main line east of Worcester, limiting their usefulness. The NYC Hudsons were also more prone to slipping than their J2 cousins, overpowering their larger driver diameter at the lower speeds typical of mountain railroading. For these reasons they were soon replaced by a number of assigned L3a Mohawks with 69 inch drivers. These engines, along with diesels from EMD, ALCO/GE, and some unfortunate Baldwins, supplemented—then replaced—the tired J2 75 inch-drivered Hudsons. Those J2s that were able migrated to the NYC Harlem and West Shore lines. Those that were not became the first System Hudsons to go for scrap.

A similar story was unfolding in freight power. In 1947 several L2a Mohawk freighters were assigned to take pressure off the A1 fleet. L4 dual service Mohawks also made occasional appearances. Their extra 1.5 inch height over the L3-class earned them the distinction of being banned east of Beacon Park.

More significantly, also in 1947, came the flowering of the seed planted in 1944 by the 1600 and her kin. Freight diesel power quickly proliferated in the form of FA1/FB1 sets from Alco and the so-called Erie-builts from Fairbanks-Morse.

These developments had the same effect on the A1 types as the changes in passenger power did on the J2s. Those A1s as could find new homes on the system did. In all, 33 Berkshires left the B&A between 1947 and 1949, never to return. The rest were white-lined by the end of 1949 with the exception of two that went to the Tennessee, Alabama & Georgia in 1950.

The NYC committed to a dieselization program soon after the war that dictated the displacement of steam power as rapidly as possible from east to west. This made sense because New England was harder on its indigenous power than the rest of the System, and was certainly the farthest afield from the fuel supply. Because of power condition and higher fuel costs (the farther east one goes) this was actually the soundest dieselization policy which could have been chosen.

Thus all serviceable steam power migrated west off the B&A as soon as it could be replaced by new diesel power. Any surviving prewar power was relettered NYC as it was displaced, in keeping with the continuing NYC policy to de-emphasize the subsidiary roads' identity and present itself to the traveling and shipping public as a single entity. Thus even the B&A's prewar high-hood Alco diesel switchers were relettered by the early 1950s.

An unusual aside to this story is the rather drawn out replacement of switchers. Steam switchers were regarded by most roads as the most eligible for quick replacement. The ratio of time-working to time-doing-nothing was abysmal. Also it was the yard engine which the city fathers saw daily blowing coal dust and smoke all over, not the passing road engine. If the yard engine was a diesel, then the smoke abatement problem would become far less visible. As public relations, the diesel switcher was perhaps more valuable than the streamlined passenger diesel. Indeed Boston got its respite very early in the dieselization game in the form of several HH600s built in 1938 by Alco, while Pittsfield didn't get diesel switchers until 1949, when five 1,000 hp Alcos were assigned in February.

The last scheduled steam powered move on the B&A was the highly publicized run of the *New England Wolverine* on April 16, 1951. L3a No. 3004 took the train west off the B&A and left behind the first major railroad in New England to be totally dieselized.

By the time this photo of No. 1207 was made on Monday, January 28, 1950, the H-5s were assigned to less important than main line duties, having been supplanted by a large diesel roster. Here the locomotive has a short freight hop at Palmer. Stephen R. Payne photo.

Boston's Suburban Tankers

The Boston and Albany was famous in the steam era not only for the pioneer 2-8-4 Berkshires but also for the 2-6-6T and 4-6-6T double-enders handling commuter traffic to and from South Station each work day.

The lineage of these engines can be drawn back to the early 0-4-4Ts built for the New York & Harlem by Schenectady Locomotive Co. in 1876. These engines introduced the Vanderbilt roads to the flexibility of a locomotive able to operate at regular speed in either direction for urban use.

By 1901 the concept had been refined with the introduction of the Class J 2-6-6T. Sixteen were placed in service between the old Grand Central and outlying points on both the Hudson and Harlem Divisions. Their useful life on the NYC was cut short when New York City banned steam traction between Grand Central and the Harlem River in 1903.

Conditions in Boston were similar because of the high volume of commuter traffic and limited space for turning facilities within the city. The double-ender concept was brought to the B&A when the NYC assumed control at the turn of the century. Indeed some of the original Class J types found their way to Boston for a short time before being withdrawn from service and rebuilt into 2-6-0 tender locomotives.

Boston got its own double-enders starting with two orders of 2-6-6T locomotives from American in Schenectady. These were almost identical to the J types and were assigned classes L1 and L1a. The L1 class, Nos. 1250-1259, was delivered starting in February 1906, while the L1a class, Nos. 1260-1267, arrived in December 1907. Both classes were lettered "New York Central Lines," irritating Bostonians at least twice daily.

In 1912 the entire B&A roster was renumbered and the offending name replaced with the original "Boston & Albany." Although there was no change in the relationship with the NYC, this was indeed a shrewd public relations gesture on the Central's part. With the change came a renumbering of the L1 class to 300-317.

The L1 class enjoyed a quiet career through the twenties,

Basic Boston & Albany 35

working in concert with some of the early K type Pacifics to cover the Boston commuter operation. They received upgrades from time to time at the road's West Springfield Shops and the class was changed, first to L2 then to L3, to avoid confusion with the Central's increasing number of L series 4-8-2 Mohawks.

By 1925 it had come to the attention of the NYC Engineering Department that the B&A 4-4-0s, 4-6-0s, and early 4-6-2s were in dire need of replacement. The long-haul travel boom of the mid-1920s also stretched the new (1925) K6 Pacifics to their practical limits almost immediately after delivery. The Central's motive power chief chose a stop-gap approach at first. Five new Hudsons, based on the NYC's superb J1 class, arrived in 1928 to help the K6 in long-haul service.

Short-haul traffic also needed new power and the NYC again elected to order a small number of new locomotives to supplement the existing fleet. Here the choice was to try an enlarged double-ender as a possible solution. The new 4-6-6T was to be as competent with local trains to Springfield and Albany as it was with bolstering the commuter fleet on the east end.

Five examples of the new D1a, numbered 400-404, were delivered by American at the same time as the new Hudsons. At 352,000 lbs. they were the largest tank engines in the United States. (While some do not consider the term "tank engine" to be correct for this configuration of tenderless locomotive, its use does conform to international engineering practice.)

Tests were immediately conducted using the powerful new engine in service between Boston and Albany, a distance of 200 miles. Although the fuel capacities were adequate for short test consists with a stop at Springfield, the D1 range limitations were unacceptable with a more typical size train. Although unsuited to road use, the new locomotives were deemed a success in suburban commuter service, and there they spent their careers.

At the end of testing the new J2 Hudsons and D1 4-6-6Ts, new conclusions were made regarding passenger power. The K6 was found to be inferior to the J2, and more of the earlier Pacifics needed replacement than originally thought. The new D1 was unsuited to road service but was a superb locomotive for suburban runs. Also, economic conditions had drastically changed, the boom of 1927 becoming the bust of 1929.

Some of the old 2-6-6Ts had already left for Lima Locomotive to be completely rebuilt in 1928, and it was decided the rest would follow. By 1931 all had returned to the B&A. They were re-classed D2a (300-309) and D2b (310-317) in 1940.

The complete rebuilding of the suburban fleet allowed for the release of the best 4-6-2s from that service. They in turn could replace the remaining 4-4-0s and 4-6-0s on local trains. These engines, along with the oldest Pacifics, were made redundant by the poor economy and were scrapped. The Hudson fleet was increased to 20 by 1931 to take charge of the heavier trains. The orphan K6 Pacifics, too large for local work and too small for the long-haul trains, went west to the Pittsburgh & Lake Erie. By the mid-1930s, B&A passenger power was completely transformed from an antique collection to a maintainable if not modern roster.

It was in this form that Boston suburban traffic was handled throughout the economic recovery of the late 1930s and the war years of the 1940s. Trains were handled predominantly by the two classes of tank engines, supplemented by Pacifics when required. Wartime service took its toll and by the late 1940s it was time to replace or rebuild the 20-year-old fleet once again.

The Central decided on complete dieselization of the B&A quite early because of the mountain profile, age of the roster, and distance from the fuel supply. Thus it was decided that the suburban fleet would be replaced and not rebuilt. By 1950 the double-enders had been retired by road switchers from Alco and Lima. Those that didn't go to scrap immediately ended their days in remote places on the NYC such as Watertown, New York, on the old Hojack Line. One of the stranger fates was that of D2a No. 305, which became "shop goat" No. X305 at the Selkirk roundhouse. This second career was over by the end of 1952, marking the end of the Boston tank engines.

Boston & Albany's Tank Engines were marvelous, beautiful machines, and they served the railroad well for 44 years. They were ideally suited to the "Circuit," commuter operation of trains from Boston to Riverside via the Highland Branch, returning the main line, as well as trains operating in the reverse order. The lack of a separate tender allowed them to run at track speed safely in either direction. They were also very popular with the B&A's frequent railfan excursions. No. 404, shown here at Riverside on Thursday, March 16, 1950, was classified as a D-1a 4-6-6T. Stephen R. Payne photo.

Right: We're bringing our westbound freight over Charlton Summit today with one of the grand B&A Berkshires, No. 1454, built by Lima in 1930, the last A-1c to come off the line, and the final one of 55 locomotives in the class. The 1400s gave yeoman service to the railroad. They were beloved by all who saw them. Photographed on Thursday, January 6, 1949 by Stephen R. Payne.

Below: B&A Hudson No. 610 leads a NYC PA-PB set on the New England States at Brighton. The 4-6-4, acting as a road helper, will be removed at Albany while the diesels will continue west to Chicago. Such helpers were often used until the end of steam in April 1951. John Morrison photo/Ralph L. Phillips collection.

Basic Boston & Albany 37

11
BOSTON: THE ROAD'S ANCHOR
South Station to Beacon Park

The train rushed on across the brown autumnal land, by wink of water and the rocky coasts, the small white towns and flaming colors and the lonely, tragic and eternal beauty of New England. It was the country of his heart's desire, the dark Helen in his blood forever burning—and now the fast approach across October land, the engine smoke that streaked back on the sharp gray air that day!

The coming on of the great earth, the new lands, the enchanted city, the approach, so smoky, blind and stifled, to the ancient web, the old grimed thrilling barricades of Boston. The streets and buildings that slid past that day with such a haunting strange familiarity, the mighty engine steaming to its halt, and the great train-shed dense with smoke and acrid with its smell and full of the slow pantings of a dozen engines, now passive as great cats, the mighty station with the ceaseless throngings of its illimitable life, and all of the murmurous, remote and mighty sounds of time forever held there in the station, together with a tart and nasal voice, a hand'sbreadth off that said: "There's hahdly time, but try it if you want."

Thomas Wolfe
OF TIME AND THE RIVER (1935)

As America's busiest rail terminal for an uninterrupted three-decade run beginning in 1899, when it opened, until it was surpassed by Grand Central in New York City, South Station was the unrivaled grande dame of American travel life. That we still have the station today is a great blessing, considering that it was half demolished in the 1970s as part of overzealous plans for so-called "urban renewal."

Perhaps because we have lived contentedly with South Station for nearly a century now, or perhaps because we have lost so many great buildings in America, we sometimes forget that this important building was never perfect, even when new. There were practical flaws, but more weighty is a certain clumsiness of scale in its massive gates-of-the-city corner entrance; the clock and the eagle are over-matched by the massive base. Had Henry Hobson Richardson not died prematurely at age 48 from nephritis in 1886, he might have been the designer instead of Shepley, Rutan, and Coolidge, his successor firm. What would it have been like, one wonders? How intriguing to imagine a South Station in the image of his masterpiece, Trinity Church. True, the South Station we know is grander and more majestic than the more prosaic North Station across town, but Richardson's touch would surely have brought about something more special. With yet another decade in his portfolio, Richardson might have made magic. Nonetheless we are especially fortunate to have South Station today, even in its reduced form. Think of the great American stations lost altogether.

Writing about South Station in his 1916 book, *Passenger Terminals and Trains*, John A. Droege commented that "The through passenger . . . is inconvenienced

Main photo: *Silhouetted by the late afternoon sun, the engineer mounts the steps to E-7 4007 to begin the westbound trip of the* New England States *in March 1966. An inbound New Haven Budd RDC is about to cross in front of us. T. J. Donahue photo.* **Insert photo:** *The westbound* New England States *passes through South Station's picturesque curve headed by two E-8s on Monday, February 22, 1960. Ben Perry photo.*

South Station's image as a magical place was certainly enhanced by this dramatic cover of a circa-1920 B&A map and guide to Boston. In addition to an excellent street map of Boston and photos of the city's landmark buildings, it provided addresses and telephone numbers for NYC ticket offices across America and in Canada. RWJ Collection.

because he must come to the middle of the station to buy his ticket, retrace his steps to the outward baggage room on the west side of the station, check his baggage and then once more retrace his steps to get to his train on track 1, 13, etc., as the case may be. It has been estimated that on the average a person must cover 1,000 ft. in this manner, and that constitutes what is perhaps the most serious detriment to this terminal." Droege also thought the movement of baggage wagons between the concourse gates and the bumpers to be dangerous to passengers. One major mistake he cited were the two loop tracks built on the station's lower level. Their radius was too short, they were limited to electric operation, and they were prohibitively expensive from waterproofing against high tide in the adjacent Fort Point Channel (see page 49).

In the years before South Station, four terminals served the railroads coming in from the south and west: the Boston & Albany and the Old Colony both had depots on Kneeland Street; the Boston & Providence had its building in Park Square; and the New York & New England was located in what is now Dewey Square. Congestion around the terminals grew more difficult with each passing year. The close proximity of freight facilities to passenger stations caused congestion. On the tracks, freight cars became stacked up, took up scarce space, and impeded passenger trains. On the street side, horse-drawn freight conveyances fought with carriages and pedestrians. The depots could hardly handle the existing number of trains, let alone contemplate future expansion. The numerous grade crossings were cumbersome and dangerous, and they brought city train speeds to a crawl.

This deteriorating situation resulted in the appointment of a special, ten-member Rapid Transit Commission. Its 300-page, 1892 report to the Legislature was a comprehensive assessment of steam railroads, streets, trolleys, and possible elevated railroads. The Commission had this to say about the situation on the south side: "Trains, in certain instances, cannot be regularly dispatched or properly brought into the stations for lack of track room, and a larger number of trains, which the services already call for and will soon imperatively demand, cannot, for the same reason, be put on. There is a needless delay of all, instead of a few, trains at the Dartmouth Street crossing of the Boston & Albany with the Providence Division of the Old Colony [there were 16 diamonds located there], while a high speed cannot be made in the three-fourths of a mile of track nearest the stations of the Central Division of the Old Colony and the New York & New England, in consequence of streets crossed at grade."

The report boldly grasped solutions to Boston's transit problems. It recommended union stations on both north and south sides (clumsily omitting the Boston & Albany, which it proposed should move into the B&P's Park Square station). It recommended that station access be accomplished on elevated rights-of-way to eliminate drawbridges. Its myriad suggestions applied ample common sense from a lay perspective, although some ideas

The imposing facade of South Station dominated Dewey Square. The two streets flanking her front are Summer Street at the left and Atlantic Avenue on the right. This is Monday, August 10, 1970, and it's 5:37 p.m., the peak of the rush hour. The terminal was still mostly intact even though look- *ing very run down. Demolition of the express buildings on Atlantic Avenue at the far right would commence two years later. About half the Summer Street facade was demolished in 1973. Alan W. Wiswall photo.*

were naive from a professional railroader's viewpoint.

The Legislature and the City of Boston took notice; politicians spoke openly and loudly about their dissatisfaction with the railroads. The Report minced no words: "If intelligent self-interest on the part of the railroad companies is wanting, then the Legislature should and must compel them to act . . . A great part of the future welfare of Boston rests in the hands of the railroad companies . . ." As the Federal Railroad Administration's South Station Project Manager Richard U. Cogswell, Jr. has aptly stated, "In reality they had a gun at their head." Fearing that civic action might get beyond their control or best interests, the Boston & Albany and the New Haven (which now controlled all railroads into Boston from the south) formed an alliance and took action. The Boston Terminal Company was chartered in 1896 to coordinate the burgeoning rail passenger traffic in Boston over these lines from the south and west.

The new building was built on a parcel of land acquired from the Commonwealth of Massachusetts, three separate railroads, and 56 individual owners at a combined cost of $9 million. The Boston Terminal Company retained George B. Francis as its Resident Engineer. His first big task was the removal of more than 200 buildings to make way for the depot. To support the new structure on land compromised by water, 43,000 pilings averaging 32.5 ft. each were driven through layers of sand, gravel, and clay. Granite from Connecticut, Maine,

Massachusetts, New Hampshire, and Rhode Island went into the new edifice, which was completed in late 1898 at a cost of some $3.6 million. Dedication was December 30, 1898. Although many New Haven trains began using the terminal on January 1, 1899, B&A operations were not transferred in until Sunday, July 23, 1899.

From the *Boston Herald* Monday, July 24, 1899:

"BOSTON & ALBANY MOVING DAY. TRAINS TRANSFERRED TO THE NEW UNION STATION. KNEELAND ST. IS DESERTED BY OFFICES OF BIG RAILROAD. FATE OF OLD BUILDING IN DOUBT; BUT MAY BE USED FOR FREIGHT. PROV. DIV. SERVICE GOES TO THE NEW TERMINAL EARLY IN SEPTEMBER. It was with no little chagrin that a number of passengers found themselves confronted by closed doors at the Kneeland St. station yesterday, and it was not until they had caught up with the times that they learned their trains awaited them at the new terminal. The first train to be delivered yesterday by the Boston & Albany at the new station was the New York Express at 6:15 a.m., and its progress through the yard was without incident. The first train dispatched was the 8:15 a.m. accommodation over the circuit."

The original building included a vast trainshed with a steel and glass roof in three spans supported by cantilevers. Its overall size was 602 ft. by 570 ft., weighing

Boston: The Road's Anchor

10,000 tons. A system of subways connected the outer ends of the platforms for baggage and express wagons.

The trainshed gradually deteriorated under the constant exposure to acidic locomotive smoke, salt air, and New England winters, and in 1920 major repairs were effected. By 1930 it was decided to remove it entirely as part of a $2.5 million rehabilitation of the whole station. The removal took 100 days, and the trainshed was replaced by umbrella-type platform roofs. At the same time, the midway was modernized, taking on the look which it kept for five decades: brick walls replaced by marble, solid departure gates erected, and terrazzo floors and a new plaster ceiling added. Into the headhouse went a new restaurant, new lunchroom, and a modernized ticket facility with an electric announcing system.

The decline of rail traffic from the Second World War onward was noticeable enough, but in 1959 a fatal blow was dealt to the prosperity of the station when the New Haven's Old Colony Division commuter trains were discontinued in June. In the early 1960s the New York Central and the New Haven held joint discussions about terminating all passenger trains at Back Bay. The plan was never effected, but the two railroads (owning 30% and 70% respectively of the Boston Terminal Corporation) sold South Station to the Boston Redevelopment Authority (BRA) in 1965 for relief from property taxes.

The BRA sold the former inbound baggage room to the U. S. Post Office which expanded its existing facilities on Dorchester Avenue. The BRA demolished the Atlantic Avenue express buildings in 1972, and began demolition of the main building in 1973, starting at the Dorchester Avenue end. About half the station facing Summer Street was taken down, making way for the new headquarters building of the engineering firm Stone & Webster.

Some time in these black days someone at the BRA decided that the still-standing—and most beautiful—section of the headhouse needed to be saved. Finally the value of the property as a transportation center had been realized. It was sold to the MBTA in August 1979. Since then South Station has undergone a major transformation into one of the most practical, useful, handsome and—most important—heavily patronized stations in America. It is a miracle of our time. The energetic crowds of rail travelers, shoppers, and lunchers make it one of the city's most vital spots. The headhouse has acquired a magnificence it was quite unaccustomed to, even decades ago. Thousands of people pass through its portals every day. It sits right on the edge of the prime business district, and the Red Line subway can now be reached by direct access from the station concourse. It benefits Boston's burgeoning commuter rail network as well as Amtrak's strong Shore Line business. Greyhound Bus operations moved here in November 1992, adjacent to Track One, and a new bus terminal and parking garage were opened in October 1995 above the terminal tracks to accommodate private bus lines serving the city. Special ramps link the bus terminal to the new Third Harbor Tunnel connecting to Logan Airport. It truly has become an intermodal transportation center.

BOSTON TERMINAL COMPANY, OCTOBER 8, 1905, LONG DISTANCE B&A TRAINS

Train	Dep.	Arr.	Track	Timetable Designation
	AM			
32		6:50	1	Chicago Mail & Express
200	7:00		46*	Mail Express (except Monday)
36		8:47	1	Atlantic Express (Chicago/Toronto)
5	9:00		13	New York Express
41	10:15		5	Berkshire Express
46		10:30	1	Southwestern Express (St. Louis)
15	10:45		13	Chicago Special
	PM			
9	12:00		13	New York Express
17	2:00		13	The Wolverine (Chicago via Michigan Central)
10		3:00	3	Chicago Special
4		3:15	1	New York Express
23	3:32		5	Albany and Western Express (Chicago)
11	4:00		13	New York Express
16		5:00	3	New England Special (Chicago via Lake Shore & Michigan Southern)
8		5:40	1	New York Express
29	6:02		13	Southwestern Express (St. Louis)
31	6:30		47*	Western Mail and Express (Chicago)
37	8:00		13	Pacific Express (Chicago/Toronto)
18		8:45	26	Southwestern Limited (St. Louis)
12		9:45	28	New York Express
13	11:15		13	New York Express (also cars to Marlboro and Fitchburg)
35	11:35		14	Albany Express (except Saturday)

*NOTE: Tracks numbered in the 40s were located on the west side of the terminal tracks, adjacent to the express buildings. These short tracks are clearly visible at the left of the photograph on pages 52-53.

Left: *The* Twentieth Century Limited *is poised to depart Track 13 at 12:58 p.m., on Sunday, December 12, 1926. A new wall, closed to the weather, would be constructed in 1930 to provide a housing for the departure gates. Carlton Parker photo from the Lawson K. Hill collection.*

Below: *This dater-die impression was made by Agent No. 6 at South Station, Monday, May 26, 1941. RWJ collection.*

Interestingly the station waiting room space also doubles as the main concourse. Arriving passengers walk directly among outbound passengers, as well as those sitting at the myriad small metal tables having a sandwich or coffee and a muffin from the stylish *Au Bon Pain*, Boston's ubiquitous cafe chain. It can be quite crowded, but it's obvious that people enjoy being here. There's a palpable sense of being part of an alive and vibrant spirit.

Comparing the Old and the New

South Station's original tracks were short, a condition limiting efficiency. Tracks 1-7 and 22-28 were 680 ft. from the bumping post to the first signal bridge, enough room (today) for a 65 ft. locomotive and six 85 ft. cars without fouling. Tracks 8-11 and 18-21 were 746 ft., enough for a seventh car. Tracks 12-17 were 926 ft., able to accommodate a 12-car train. When longer trains were necessary, they fouled parts of the Tower 1 interlocking during their dwell time, a compromising situation for such a busy terminal.

Typically B&A trains used tracks 1-7 for local service, and variously tracks 12, 13, and 14 for the longer long-distance trains (with occasional exceptions). The list, opposite left, of B&A through trains is extracted from the October 8, 1905 BOSTON TERMINAL COMPANY'S ARRIVAL AND DEPARTURE OF TRAINS. Note that Trains 12 and 18 arrived on tracks 26 and 28. Possibly these trains carried large amounts of mail more easily handled on the east side of the depot. Trains 200 and 31 were mail and express trains arriving and departing from the express area on tracks 46

Total South Station Weekday Arrivals and Departures 1904-1995

	1904	1914	1918	1934	1941	1945	1950	1954	1957	1960	1966	1971	1975	1987	1995
B&A trains	218	209	172	165	131	130	84	83	54	22	18	8	12*	33	36
NH trains	643	481	434	265	188	209	152	244	212	83	90	78	96	143	202
Total trains	861	690	606	430	319	339	236	327	266	105	108	86	108	176	238

*Includes revived *Lake Shore Limited* beginning October 31, 1975

Note: New Haven RR commuter services came under MBTA funding in April 1966; Penn Central (to Framingham) in August 1973. B&M took over southside operations from Conrail in March 1977. Amtrak began operating all Boston commuter trains in January 1987.

Boston: The Road's Anchor

BOSTON SOUTH STATION

As opened January 1, 1899: 28 tracks

Configuration in 1996: 13 tracks

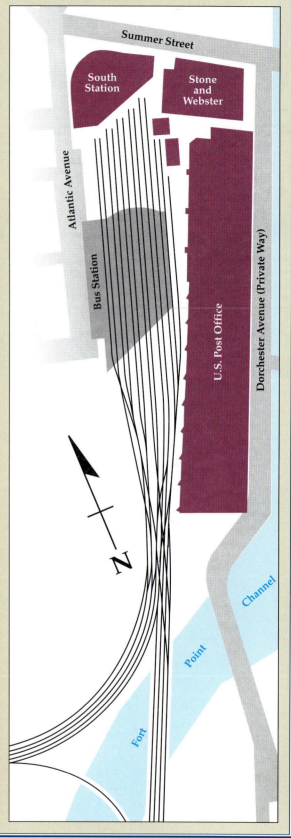

Two key factors have made longer track lengths possible in the new South Station. First, with only 13 tracks instead of the original 28, the interlocking has been simplified. Second, the land once occupied by the express building and its 12 tracks is now used for terminal tracks. The present plant can handle 400 trains a day with as many as 50 trains an hour during peak periods.

Note how the track grid was parallel to Dorchester Avenue in the original design, while today it is parallel to Atlantic Avenue.

Of the three rolling lift bridges spanning Fort Point Channel in 1899 (carrying six tracks), only two have been used regularly in recent times. The lift bridges, which have not been raised for marine navigation in many decades, are expected to be replaced by a single fixed span. First a temporary bridge is to be utilized in conjunction with Boston's Central Artery project, while later a permanent fixed span will be constructed, carrying as many as five tracks. In the meantime, the two operational bridges have been reinforced at a cost of $1.5 million to expedite safe and timely rail operation of the revived Old Colony commuter service scheduled to begin in the fall of 1997.

Our diagram at right of the tracks crossing the Fort Point Channel is based upon several MBTA track charts which envision four tracks on the present lift bridges.

Some discussion has been conducted about whether the Post Office might eventually relocate its facility, restoring the land to South Station usage at some future time. The plant will be at capacity with the opening of Old Colony service.

South Station diagrams by Dean Sauvola.

Maps © 1997 by Pine Tree Press

44 Boston & Albany

and 47, where there were no passenger loading facilities.

South Station retained its 28-track capacity until sometime after World War II, when train frequency declined quickly. The South Postal Annex building was erected over tracks 22-28 about 1934 (note the photograph on the rear end-sheet), probably causing a ventilation problem since tracks 26-28 were not used thereafter. Tracks 18-25 were out of service by the early 1960s. Tracks 1-7 were removed in the late 1960s, and although tracks 4, 5, and 6 were reinstalled by the MBTA in the mid 1970s, they were infrequently used for revenue service.

When the plant was redesigned in the 1980s, provision was made for 11 tracks. All are considerably longer because of the simplified interlocking and removal of the express buildings. High-level platforms were made possible by lowering the roadbed as much as four feet during the reconstruction (when the lower level loop tunnel was finally removed). Though some advocated a larger number of tracks, those entrusted with the decision concluded that 11 tracks could comfortably handle 400 daily trains and as many as 50 per hour at peak times. Subsequently it was decided to add tracks 12 and 13, intended for short trains such as the Dorchester Branch shuttle or the loading and unloading of mail cars. These 13 tracks completely take up the available land, all space to the east now being occupied by Post Office facilities.

In order to maximize the length of the station platform tracks, several crossovers were placed west of the big curve at "Cove" interlocking. Also, the designers of the new track layout have taken great care to provide a maximum of five simultaneous parallel moves in and out of the station. The importance of such planning will be appreciated in future years as the number of routes served by the MBTA increases.

Right: This early 1905 postcard view of South Station shows the elevated which hosted trains until September 30, 1938, and was torn down for a World War II scrap drive in June 1942. RWJ collection.

Below: The Twilight Express is ready to leave for New York City from Track 12 on Saturday, July 10, 1926. The massive trainshed would last just four more years. Carlton Parker photo from the Lawson K. Hill collection.

Above: The CHECKMAN and STATION AGENT hat badges are believed to date from before 1900, while the BAGGAGEMAN badge may be from the early 1930s. Courtesy of Michael J. Sullivan/Brian Solomon photos.

Boston: The Road's Anchor 45

Previous spread: A pink sky casts a gossamer light over the South Station interlocking, seen from Tower No. 1 in March 1966. A B&A Framingham local behind an E-7 is rounding the curve to the right while headlights and signals sparkle in the distance. T. J. Donahue photo. *Above:* During a morning rush-hour in February 1965, a B&A commuter train from Framingham enters South Station at right with a long string of the famous "turtle-back" coaches. A train of New Haven Budd RDCs is also arriving, and the semaphores and switches tell us that it will berth close to the B&A train. Fred Matthews photo. *Below:* For several years beginning in the late 1960s the station functioned without tracks 1-7, which were torn up. Trackside the decay and filth are sadly obvious. The late-afternoon winter sun casts long ghostly shadows from the vintage baggage wagons. Allan H. Wiswall photo.

THE INFAMOUS LOOP AND ITS LEGACY

The idea for a lower level to handle suburban trains was given its impetus in the 1892 Rapid Transit Commission *Report* (see page 40), based on one commissioner's observation of London suburban train operation. As planned, electrified commuter trains would have been able to enter the double-track loop, load or unload, and leave quickly. The dwell time could possibly have been as short as two minutes. The design (the maximum radius of the loop) was restricted by the site's size. It was designed to accommodate 50 ft. cars (patterned after Nantasket Beach prototypes), and electrification was imperative. Each loop track could have accommodated seven electric-locomotive-pulled three-car trains.

Old-time South Station employees long embraced the legend of a steam train pulling into the underground loop for the first and last time, driving out a choking crowd of invited guests. Overlooked is the fact that railroad officials involved in South Station's construction and operation had stated repeatedly that the loop tracks were intended only for future electrification or other smokeless propulsion systems. Surely such a grand opening ceremony would not be held without the benefit of a test train which would have immediately demonstrated the impossibility of steam in the tunnel.

The loop tracks were never used, but the more significant damage was the failure to electrify the suburban lines. For decades Boston remained ambivalent about how it might upgrade its suburban rail lines. The conversion of the New Haven's Shawmut branch into the rapid transit to Ashmont in 1928, paralleling the Old Colony tracks 2.4 miles between Andrew and Fields Corner, was deemed a success. Logically people contemplated what additional rail lines might be converted to electric operation and able to feed directly into the downtown subway system. In April 1945, in its report to the Massachusetts Legislature, the Coolidge Commission proposed to extend Boston's rapid transit system to radiate 12 miles from the center of the city.

The July-August 1945 issue of *The Railroad Enthusiast* summarized the report: "The plans call for the operation of PCC cars on some routes and rapid transit trains on others over the rails of present steam roads and directly into the downtown subways thereby eliminating local railroad passenger service . . . It is understood that railroad freight service will continue on these branches as on others, making it necessary for the new service to overpass sidings, spurs, etc."

The concept was advanced in 1954 with the completion of the Metropolitan Transit Authority (MTA) East Boston line from Maverick Square to Wonderland (today's Blue Line). This was built partly on the right-of-way of the narrow-gauge Boston, Revere Beach & Lynn which ceased operation in January 1940.

A much more major project was the 1958 conversion of the B&A Highland Branch into one piece of today's MBTA Green Line. This line was unique among Boston commuter lines in that its 12 stations were within a 9-mile distance (from the junction with the main line). It was cumbersome to operate conventional rail equipment with such close station spacing, and its status as a dense, upper-class suburban area made it environmentally extra-sensitive. Thus the conversion to electric light rail was ideal: no appreciable engine noise, smaller crews, and the resulting greater frequency.

The next implementation of the rail conversion plan was to have been the Old Colony as far as Quincy. It was delayed until the MTA was replaced in 1964 by the Massachusetts Bay Transportation Authority (MBTA), with an expanded jurisdiction to 78 cities and towns. Four years of construction concluded when the new line opened to Quincy Center in September 1970, eleven years after the Old Colony's shut-down.

As the next big project came closer to implementation— converting the B&M's Reading line into an extension of the Orange Line—it faltered, and for good reason. A ground swell of local support forced a change in thinking, so that instead of *replacing* the B&M line, the Orange Line was squeezed onto the same corridor. The Commonwealth then made a firm commitment to commuter rail, now thriving in Boston. The restoration of two of three Old Colony lines— dormant since 1959—is imminent in 1997.

Two major challenges still face Massachusetts. First, the inclusion of a rail right-of-way inside the proposed Central Artery Tunnel is not a sure thing. The major cost will not be the tunnel itself, but rather providing the connections to the tunnel at North and South Stations, with new lower-level stations at both locations. Such a tunnel would enable through-running trains. Second, the electrification of the commuter rail lines would effect a more efficient, cleaner operation. A *Boston Globe* story on May 16, 1993 listed route pairings then under consideration in an electrified, through tunnel: Fitchburg-Lakeville; Lowell-Stoughton; Haverhill-Providence; North Wilmington-Needham Heights; Newburyport-Worcester; Beverly-Forge Park; and Rockport-Plymouth (Readville and Greenbush segments were left terminated in Boston). And it would permit Amtrak service through Boston to the north.

Paris, France serves as an interesting comparison to Boston. Its famous Métro was found to be inadequate by the 1960s. The city's bold solution was to create the RER (Regional Express System). Its high-level cars travel under Paris in new tunnels at much deeper levels than the Métro and stop at stations which are much farther apart (some are dual Métro-RER stations). RER trains travel outside Paris on former suburban railroad lines. They are built for long-distance comfort, compared to the simpler Métro cars which function as a typical city subway. The RER provides the advantage of high-speed, long-distance commuter service, while the Métro provides more intensive in-city coverage.

Connecting Boston's north- and south-side rail operations through the Central Artery Tunnel would bring a similar and welcome fluidity and efficiency to MBTA Commuter Rail. It would require electrification of the commuter rail network in order to be fully practical, and it would fulfill the most visionary proposal of the 1892 Rapid Transit Commission *Report*.

Left: *A wonderfully contrasted study of steel trains, rails, and signals at South Station in the mid-1940s by the late H. W. Pontin, B&A engineman and lifetime railfan and photographer. This is perhaps Train 23, a Springfield local, departing from Track 3. Today's power is B&A Hudson No. 601. J. W. Swanberg collection.*

Above right: *South Station's midway was quiet this Sunday, January 26, 1969, at 3:15 p.m. Most of the concessions are shut for the weekend; many shops closed after the 1959 cessation of New Haven Old Colony service. Leaks in the ceiling indicate a lack of maintenance by its owner, the Boston Redevelopment Authority.*

Right: *The bank of ticket windows featured an ornate, clean design in the brass grillwork. The metalwork trim around the windows is quite stylish. Note the New York Central poster for "Sleepercoach" service at right.*

Far right: *A close-up detail of Window 7, one of several serving the New Haven. B&A windows were to the far left. The large "C" in the upper left corner was part of the word "TICKETS" on the wall. Three photos by Allan H. Wiswall.*

Below left: *No. 810 was a 600-hp switcher built by Alco-GE in 1939 as Boston & Albany No. 684. It was renumbered 810 in 1948, then re-lettered New York Central in 1952. On Friday, May 24, 1957 it was moving a baggage car on the curve just outside South Station. William T. Clynes photo.*

Below right: *NYC E-8 4072 will depart soon with a single coach for Albany, the inexcusably sad remnant of the New England States. In the background is New Haven train No. 29, the Gilt Edge, for New York City. Behind it is the South Postal Annex, built in the mid-1930s. The date is Sunday, January 26, 1969. Note the missing tracks in the foreground. Allan H. Wiswall photo.*

Boston: The Road's Anchor   51

Left: This ten-ticket strip (Nos. 1-3 have already been torn off and used) of shoe shine tickets provided employees the opportunity to have a 5¢ shine—presumably a discount price—at any of M. J. McAloon's stands at South Station. When all coupons were used up, another strip was issued "upon application." This was a good incentive to encourage employees to maintain a proper shine always. Norton D. Clark collection.

Above: Allan H. Wiswall made this photo of the *New England States* from Tower No. 1 on September 17, 1961, a Sunday, which explains why there are only two other trains in sight. Departure time is 3:40 p.m. This shot captures the sense of occasion about the *States* as it prepared for departure on track 13. Noting that the two E-7s at left are facing backward, we can deduce there was at least one other to the front. There are 17 tracks in place, though the last shows considerable rusting and has no access platform. To the right we see where tracks have been removed and a bulldozer has been leveling the land. The *States* carried three sleepers (one a "Sleepercoach") to Chicago, one sleeper each to Toronto and Cleveland, a diner, a tavern car, and coaches. At Albany the train added two more Chicago sleepers and one for Pittsburgh. The New Haven train at the right is No. 31, the 4:00 p.m. *Gilt Edge* for New York City.

Above: *The miraculous rebirth of South Station is vibrantly illustrated by this July 1990 view of the lunch crowd in the new main concourse. At center is the popular Au Bon Pain which has numerous locations in Boston. The ticket offices are in the distance at right.*

Left: *This is the new track layout as seen from the cab of a Providence-Boston MBTA train entering South Station's throat in August 1992 during the early evening. Five simultaneous parallel moves are possible.*

Above: This overview of the new trackage was made in July 1992 from the fifth-floor bathroom of Amtrak's South Station offices. Today a bus terminal/parking structure occupies the space above the tracks and this open view is no longer possible. Also, two additional tracks have been added on the left side to make a total of 13. The South Postal Annex, at left, is built on land once entirely covered with station tracks. Its relocation to a different site would alleviate South Station's long-term capacity difficulties. The restoration of Old Colony commuter service is expected to fill the station's present track capacity at rush hour. *Below:* MBTA's smart silver-burgundy-yellow paint scheme is seen to best advantage on bright sunny days such as this spectacular summer morning in August 1992. Note the lack of roofs to protect passengers from the weather. The square boxes between the tracks are the tops of foundation piles for the bus terminal/parking structure. Four photos by RWJ.

Boston: The Road's Anchor   55

Winter lingers past its welcome this April 1960 day as a lone NYC Budd RDC is outbound on Track 3 through the falling snow near Trinity Place station. Buried in the snow are four B&A and four NH tracks. At Back Bay station, just ahead, the New Haven's tracks will turn southwest for Providence, New Haven, and New York City. The Knickerbocker Beer billboard sits above the "town" end of NH Back Bay station. The layout here will change dramatically in a few years with the coming of the Massachusetts Turnpike Extension. In the distance a Main Line Elevated train is crossing high overhead (after 1966 it would be called the Orange Line). Fred Matthews photo.

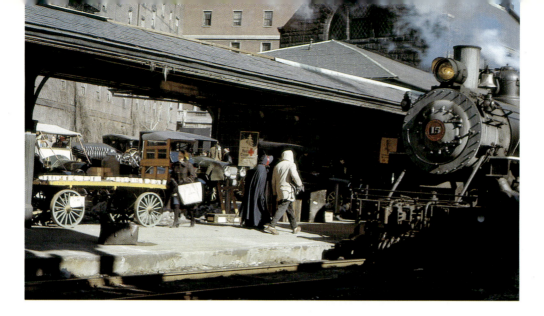

Above and left: For the filming of The Cardinal *starring the late Tom Tryon, producer Otto Preminger engaged Monadnock Northern to bring its No. 15 to Boston for the film shoot, shown here with set decorations at Trinity Place on Saturday, February 16, 1963. The 2-8-0 locomotive is ex-Rahway Valley. Two photos by Allan H. Wiswall.*

Below: NYC E-7 No. 4023 brings the New England States *into Trinity Place in April 1961 in a fine view of the depot. Both Trinity Place and Huntington Avenue (opposite) stations were designed in 1899 by A. W. Longfellow, who served as a senior draftsman to Henry Hobson Richardson from 1882 to 1886. Fred Matthews photo.*

Below: Boston-Trinity Place ticket from the Preston Johnson collection.

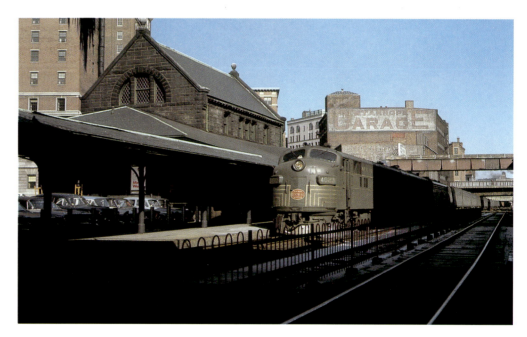

58   Boston & Albany

Above: NYC S-1 switcher No. 847 (Alco-GE 660 hp) is hauling the consist of the *New England States* past Huntington Avenue station toward Beacon Park for overnight servicing. The railroad built two separate stations at this location—Trinity Place and Huntington Avenue—cater-corner to each other, because of the limited space available. Both were fully functional into the 1950s, except that there was no ticket agent at Huntington Avenue, since it served only inbound trains. It has been boarded up in this Friday, November 23, 1962 photo. The brick building behind the depot is the New Haven's Back Bay Station. *Below:* In this view taken a few moments later, the Exeter Street Yard is gone, and the new Prudential Tower is well under way. The railroad will be rerouted two portals to the left, while its present roadbed will be occupied by the Massachusetts Turnpike Extension. The little Tower No. 6 in the center hasn't got long. Two photos by Russell F. Munroe.

Boston: The Road's Anchor

Above left: *This 1965 view from the top of the Prudential Tower provides a dramatic overview of the Massachusetts Turnpike Extension and how the B&A's tracks were reduced to make room. The New England States has stopped at Back Bay for westbound passengers, and can be seen clearly at the bottom of the photo. Back Bay Station has since been replaced with an MBTA and Amtrak station which serves both the former B&A and NH*

rails, as well as the Orange Line which opened here in 1987. **Left:** In the summer of 1965 a B&A commuter train to Framingham is powered by NYC E-8 No. 4076, and is running alongside the Massachusetts Turnpike Extension just east of Back Bay Station (as the B&A's stop is now called). Compare this photo with that on pp. 56-57. Two photos by Fred Matthews. **Above:** Late on a summer afternoon in 1950, Alco RS-2 No. 8222 waits with a standard-coach consist (most likely a Worcester train) at the Exeter Street Yard in Boston's Back Bay. All three trains will soon back into South Station for passenger loading. Judging from the number of cars stored here, this is still a busy railroad. Today the Prudential Center completely occupies this site, while the railroad passes under in a two-track tunnel adjacent to the Massachusetts Turnpike Extension. Russell F. Munroe photo.

Boston: The Road's Anchor   61

YARDS AND ENGINES
PAUL T. CARVER

The heart of any railroad is not just its main line but its yards and engine facilities which make possible the limiteds and fast freights. The original land of the B&A's Kneeland Street station lay just west of today's South Station complex. After the creation of South Station in 1899, the rail trackage here served as loading areas for express, Pacemaker, and some freight car operations right up to the 1970s.

At mp 1.43, the Exeter Street Yards (adjacent to Huntington Avenue in Back Bay) served as suburban coach and passenger car yards, and dining car commissary. Here whole trains were stored, cleaned, and prepared for the next trip west from South Station. Switchers, suburban double-enders and, later, diesel road switchers handled these moves.

The B&A's Boston engine terminal for steam years, after the move to South Station in 1899, was at Beacon Park. Its eastern end is at Grand Junction, mp 3.32 (Tower 9). Its western end is at Allston, mp 4.24 (Tower 10) and the Cambridge Street bridge, a nearly mile-long section trapped between the main line and the Charles River. In full swing in the 1920s, 30s, and 40s, its two roundhouses and turntables were converted to servicing diesels in the 1950s. The last scheduled steam was Mohawk 3004 leaving Boston for Chicago on the *Wolverine* April 16, 1951. In steam's last years, with the demise of Beacon Park's high coaling towers, coaling was accomplished with a clamshell crane. Engine servicing of Conrail power today is a mere shadow of the former operation.

Associated with the Beacon Park terminal were the Allston yards with a 55-track, 2,500-freight car capacity. They served as a collection point for all the B&A's Boston's sidings, the Grand Junction Branch and its piers on Boston Harbor, as well as connections with the Boston & Maine and New Haven Railroads. More than three-quarters of these yards have disappeared, taken over by the Massachusetts Turnpike and its truck parks. However, increasing trucking now arrives by intermodal rail, the virtual staple of rail freight activity today on the B&A. Business here is an unqualified success.

In Conrail years in the late 1970s, the two-ended yards consisted of some 22 tracks, several arrival-departure tracks, a loading facility, and an abbreviated engine service terminal.

At Riverside, junction of the main line and west end of the Highland Branch, the B&A maintained a coach yard, engine facilities, and a turntable, all removed in the late fifties.

To the west, Newtonville had a small yard and Framingham a medium-sized one. Worcester, a major junction with the B&M and NH, had both large passenger and freight yards, as well as extensive engine servicing facilities.

Left: Behind E-7 No. 4015, plus an E-8 and another E-7, the New England States is just west of Massachusetts Avenue and headed for Chicago in the Fall of 1962. The train's consist includes both smooth-sided and stainless steel cars. Two tracks have already been removed for Turnpike construction. Fred Matthews photo.

Above: Many refer to this massive passenger storage facility as the Huntington Avenue Yard, but its official name was Exeter Street Yard. Exeter Street is behind the photographer; Boylston Street is at upper right. Huntington Avenue is out of sight at the left (the photo on pp. 60-61 shows a row of buildings in the right background on Huntington Avenue). Most of the rolling stock here are suburban coaches. The stainless steel cars at upper right are for the through trains. Note the Union Pacific and Pennsylvania Railroad Pullmans at the right. The B&A dining car commissary was also located here. August 1958 photo by Donald M. Fellows/Charles M. Abraham, Jr. collection.

Above right: The B&A's venerable fleet of 80 Osgood Bradley suburban coaches was numbered 300-379 and built 1924-28. They were not air conditioned but came equipped with ceiling fans for the hot summer days. The rattan seats were spartan but very durable, as were the passengers since these cars were built without restrooms. The cars had three steps rather than the standard two on most railroads, with the bottom step just 12 inches off a rail-height platform. They were renumbered in the 1100 series between 1953 and 1957 and relettered for the New York Central. The last were retired in 1971.

Below right: The Osgood Bradley coaches wore the drabbest of dark greens and were especially grim looking on gray days, such as this wintry Saturday, January 23, 1960, at Beacon Park. Note the B&A initials built into the chimney with white brick, a once-common practice in New England. Two photos by Allan H. Wiswall.

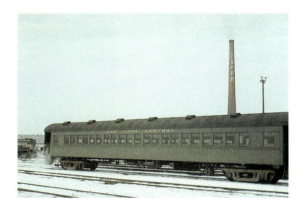

Boston: The Road's Anchor 63

Below: This red globe lantern was manufactured by the C. T. Ham Co., probably in the 1880s. It is thought to have been an engine lamp, possibly an early classification light. Note the raised B&A initials. The lantern is in the collection of Michael J. Sullivan. Brian Solomon photo.

64 Boston & Albany

Left: On Saturday, June 15, 1946, NYC Class L-3a 4-8-2 No. 3008 leads Train 49, the Knickerbocker, west from Boston along the Charles River near the B&A's Beacon Park yard in Allston. John Morrison photo/Ralph L. Phillips collection.

Below left: The famous New England States, Train 27, is behind double-headed steam with a J-2 Hudson in the lead, this Sunday, October 14, 1945 at Beacon Park. In the lower left can be seen part of B&A Tank Engine No. 401. F. Rodney Dirkes photo/RWJ collection.

Above right: At the same location 25 years later we see major changes in the trackwork. Two of four main line tracks have been annexed into the yard, and the Massachusetts Turnpike Extension is very much in evidence. Note the preponderance of intermodal trains. The switchers are both Alco-GE 1,000 hp Model S-2 locomotives. No. 9607 was built in February 1944 as No. 788, becoming No. 8508 later that year, and No. 9607 in 1966. No. 9613 was built in November 1944 as No. 8521 and renumbered as No. 9613 in 1966. Leon Onofri collection.

Center right: Long after B&A steam vanished from the railroad, Monadnock Northern No. 15 graces the Beacon Park turntable on Saturday, February 16, 1963, the same day as its film shoot at Trinity Place, shown on p. 58. Allan H. Wiswall photo.

Below right: The Beacon Park engine terminal remained a busy operation after steam. No. 1034 is an FA-1 built by Alco in May 1949. This day in June 1961 the locomotive heads a five-unit set for freight service. At left is E-7 No. 4011, a 1947 product of General Motors. At right is an E-8A—E-7B—E-8A passenger set. John F. Kane photo.

Boston: The Road's Anchor 65

GRAND JUNCTION BRANCH

On Sunday, May 3rd, just 100 members and friends of the New England Division braved the elements to make our first trip of the season over the B&A. The group left South Station . . . in a special train consisting of suburban type locomotive No. 402 and coaches 488, 476, and 539 . . . At 3:45 the train resumed its course, moving over the nine miles of the Grand Junction branch, thru East Cambridge, where more than 100 side tracks serve that extensive industrial district, and then thru Somerville, Everett, and Chelsea to the terminal at East Boston [where] the party viewed the two waterfront terminal yards, having capacity for more than 1,000 cars, the seven-storied fireproof storage warehouse, the grain elevator, and the four piers where steamers of the Cunard White Star and other lines dock.

Cyrus Hosmer, Jr.
THE ENTHUSIAST (July 1936)

The Grand Junction's first moniker was the Chelsea Branch Railroad Company, incorporated in 1846. The name was changed to the Grand Junction Railroad & Depot Company in 1847. Information in a Grand Junction annual report suggests it opened in December 1851. When the company arranged to charter the Union Railroad for another three miles to a connection with the Boston & Worcester across the Charles River in Cottage Farm, Brookline, the B&W purchased $100,000 of its bonds in 1853. This trackage was completed in 1855, giving the B&W its long-sought port access, as well as connections to all four northern railroads: Fitchburg, Boston & Lowell, Boston & Maine, and the Eastern. The B&W's financial participation provided it the opportunity to lease wharves in East Boston. The Grand Junction—actually a front for land speculators—went bankrupt in 1857, complicating the B&W's wharf lease. The B&W's directors refused more money for the project, unenthusiastic about carrying the Western Railroad's bulky freight over their rails, and they sought remedies in court. The tracks between Somerville and Brookline went unused during years of litigation. All the while the B&W depended on the cumbersome horse-and-wagon freight transfer between its depot and South Cove. It wasn't until 1869 that the newly formed Boston & Albany, under President Chapin, finally unraveled the whole mess and enabled the railroad to have its long cherished deep water port.

Coloring Chapin's action were the efforts of the Grand Junction's backers who had succeeded in getting the New York & Boston (the so-called "Air Line," coming into Boston on what would later become the B&A's Highland Branch) interested in the Grand Junction as a strategic link to railroads to the north and the port at East Boston. A legislative bill, passed earlier in 1866, enabled takeover by the B&W, later consummated by the B&A.

Interestingly part of the branch in Revere and Chelsea was used by the Eastern Railroad to bring its mainline into a Causeway Street station in Boston, to replace its earlier ferry connection from East Boston. The Eastern used these tracks from 1854 until its own parallel tracks were added several years later. Crossing the Mystic River along this section was Draw 7, a three-track bridge used by the Boston & Maine and the B&A, built in 1894 and used until 1989. The B&M used two tracks, the B&A the third. The last train to use Draw 7 was MBTA Train 145, a commuter train to Rockport, leaving Boston at 12:06 a.m., Saturday, August 26, 1989. The bridge's closure followed the completion of a new, taller, double-track, fixed span a few hundred feet to the west, which also accommodates any Conrail moves.

The Grand Junction hosted weekly trains in the 1870s and 1880s to transport immigrants directly from arriving ships to points in the West, the only known scheduled passenger trains on these rails. The May 28, 1899 B&A Employee Timetable shows seven scheduled freights on the branch, including a daily milk train from Barre Plains on the Ware River Branch going to Massachusetts Avenue, and a B&M freight between Chelsea and East Boston.

The many trains on the Grand Junction were a terrible annoyance to local residents because of the many grade crossings. Complaints to the city fathers became so rampant that the 1892 *Report of the Rapid Transit Commission* called for closure of the branch and recommended that the B&A conduct all its waterfront activities at the South Boston docks (the report also offered that the Boston & Maine "needed" the B&A's East Boston wharf and elevator property). Alternatively the report suggested the B&A reach East Boston by building a new line from Riverside along the Charles River to the Fitchburg Railroad near Roberts, about two miles. This would have ameliorated the grade crossing problem but it would have also deprived the railroad of enormous freight revenues from on-line business in Cambridge.

In 1909 the *Report of the Commission on Metropolitan Improvements* described the Grand Junction as "owned and operated by one railroad corporation through territory logically and geographically belonging to another system," a none-too-subtle suggestion that the B&M had its eyes on the property. The same report noted that, in the two-and-one-half-mile space between Massachusetts Avenue in Cambridge and Broadway in Somerville, the Grand Junction crossed eight streets, nine trolley tracks,

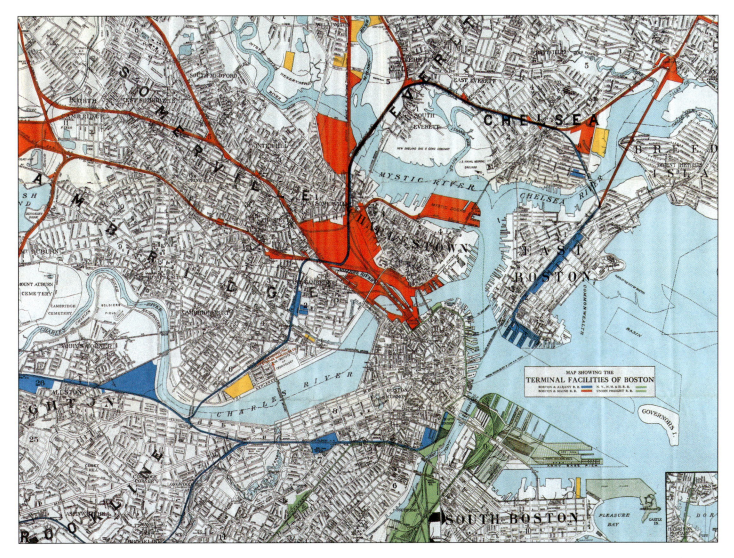

The New Haven Railroad published this map of commercial Boston showing clearly how the major railroads interacted. The Boston & Albany's Grand Junction Branch—blue—virtually bisects the Boston & Maine—red—in Somerville. The New Haven and Union Freight Railroads are shown in green. The complete map covers more area than is shown here, and was published in the era circa 1920. RWJ collection.

eight mainline railroad tracks, and nine sidings—all at grade. In the same space there were 22 *former* grade crossings which now ended at the Grand Junction right-of-way. The B&A served 42 separate manufacturing companies on the branch. No wonder the B&M wanted it.

Other sources differ regarding the number of industries and sidings. An 1897 map from the Warren Jacobs collection shows 29 sidings between Cottage Farm and Somerville Avenue. A 1908 B&A brochure noted the presence of 65 large industries on the branch between East Boston and Cottage Farm, 55 of them with private side tracks, plus another hundred receiving or sending freight. Cyrus Hosmer, Jr. reported seeing more than 100 sidings serving industry on the entire branch when he passed over it in 1936 with an excursion sponsored by The Railroad Enthusiasts, Inc. Whatever the exact numbers, the Grand Junction was far and away the B&A's most profitable branch.

A major fire on July 8, 1908 destroyed the grain elevator and three of four piers at the B&A's East Boston Terminal. Its $4 million replacement opened two years later with completely fireproofed buildings and piers. The whole facility included two waterfront terminal yards with capacity for more than 1,000 cars, a seven-story storage warehouse, a grain elevator, and four piers.

The 1909 *Report* considered the Grand Junction to be as close to a "belt-line" as Boston would ever have, given the staggering cost of building a real one around the city. Suggestions for completely double-tracking the branch were made, but not all were carried out. When the separate highway and railroad bridges at Cottage Farm were rebuilt about 1910, double track was provided. It continued all the way to the B&M's Fitchburg Division, which was crossed by a single track, becoming double again behind the Boston Engine Terminal. The B&A reverted to single track to cross the B&M's Western and Eastern Divisions, becoming double iron at B&M Tower C. It was single track over Draw 7, then double

Boston: The Road's Anchor   67

GRAND JUNCTION FREIGHT SIDINGS IN 1897

A hand-drawn map dated August 16, 1897 from the Warren Jacobs collection lists the following industrial sidings on the Grand Junction Branch. We are indebted to Peter T. Victory for further research on these businesses in the 1897 *Cambridge City Directory* in the Special Collections of the Massachusetts State Library, Boston.

East Main

- Armstrong track (possibly Riverside Press)*
- Walker Oil track*
- John P. Squire Co. hog track
    (pork, lard, tripe, sausages, pigs' feet, bacon, ham, and extra lard oil)
- John P. Squire Co. salt track
- John P. Squire Co. straight track
- Geopper*
- Dennis Thompson Coal track*
- American Rubber Co.
    (rubber surface clothing, macintoshes, etc.)
- Riverside Oil track*
- Cambridgeport siding
- Page Produce yard*
- Storage track

*No listings for these businesses in 1897 *Directory*

West Main

- North Packing & Provision Co. track
    (pure leaf lard, hams, bacon, dry salted and pickled meats, barrel pork, pure lard, and sausages)
- North Packing & Provision Co. hog track
- North Packing & Provision Co. market track
- Side track
- David W. Lewis (sewer pipe)
- Page Portland Street yard*
- Chelmsford Foundry (wrought and cast iron)
- Boston Woven Hose and Rubber Co. No. 2
    (rubber goods, hose, tires, belts, and packing)
- Boston Woven Hose and Rubber Co. No. 1
- Mason & Hamlin (piano manufacturer)
- Page Harvard Street yard*
- George W. Gale Co. (lumber)
- Long siding
- John Reardon & Sons (soap manufacturer)
- Norcross Bros. (stone cutters)
- Dearborn*

---

all the way to the East Boston terminus. The *Report* also called for lowering the Grand Junction under the B&M's Fitchburg route to follow a different alignment, going west and north of the McLean Asylum property, land where the B&M eventually built its classification yard, also envisioned in the *Report*. But the Grand Junction has kept its B&M grade crossing ever since; indeed a new diamond was installed in 1995 after several years of using crossover switches.

The Chelsea Creek drawbridge was closed in 1955 when its counterweight collapsed into the creek on February 28, taking the approach tracks with it. Robert A. Buck remembers his friend Albert Smith, a former B&A crossing tender, once saying, "You know, every time I pushed the 'down' button on that bridge I waited for it to keep going. A week after I left the job and the regular man came back, it did." After that, trains going to East Boston used a two-and-one-half-mile longer route on the B&M via Revere, the original route of the Eastern Railroad to East Boston. Ironically the bridge which collapsed in 1955 was a replacement for a "jack knife" type drawbridge which collapsed in November 1906.

Today Conrail uses the line only as far as a produce center in Everett, on the site of the former Eastern Gas & Fuel, while several grade crossings further on are paved over. In October 1995 Conrail donated one mile of its for-

Left: *Tower E-5 at Everett Junction controlled the switches of the B&A going into the railroad of the Eastern Gas & Fuel Co., also known as the "Coke Works." The EG&F had a number of its own locomotives. The B&A paralleled the B&M on single track from Tower C through Draw 7, then double track past Tower E-5 all the way to East Boston. The Tower, depicted here on Sunday, May 24, 1970, was on the south side of the B&M at the Coke Works Junction. Norton D. Clark collection.*

Right: In August 1958 NYC caboose No. 17014 (former B&A) accompanies a Pennsylvania RR Pullman on the Grand Junction near the MIT power plant. The sleeper was most likely on its way north to some luxurious summer spa on the Boston & Maine.
Donald M. Fellows photo/Charles M. Abraham, Jr. collection.

mer right-of-way in East Boston for the city to create a greenway linking several parks.

The Grand Junction assumed a new role when the B&M began running the southside commuter trains in 1977, and it was necessary to move commuter rail equipment between North and South Stations for maintenance. The MBTA engaged Amtrak to operate all Boston commuter trains in 1987, and today the Grand Junction sees several daily movements of deadheading commuter rail trains.

Above: The B&A's grain elevator was near the debarkation site for thousands of steamship travelers from overseas throughout the years. In 1955 it was leased to the Continental Grain Company which initiated large exports of U. S. grain overseas. A shipment that July of 850,000 bushels of barley—from Buffalo and beyond—was the largest single shipment to move through the Port of Boston up to that time. B&A work cars X-2186 and X-2185 sit in front of the grain elevator on January 1, 1965. Norton D. Clark collection.

Boston: The Road's Anchor

Left: *Draw 7 was the last operating example in the eastern U. S. of a once-popular design of a horizontally folding drawbridge, sometimes called a "jackknife" bridge. The technology was patented by Joseph Ross of Ipswich in 1849. It was built in conjunction with the opening of the new Union Station in 1894, when seven of eight original drawbridges were replaced. Draw 7 carried three tracks: two for the B&M and one (on the east side) for the B&A. The original bridge was built in 1849-50 by the Grand Junction Railroad and Depot Company, and substantially rebuilt in 1858 by the Eastern Railroad. The Eastern depended on the bridge for its new Causeway Street terminal access at a time when the Grand Junction was insolvent and unable to pay, and had stopped using the track.*

The mechanisms of the bridge raised the girders three inches on the far side, then swung them sideways until they reached a right angle from their closed position, clearing a 42 ft. channel for Mystic River navigation. Throughout the life of the bridge, the B&A paid one-third its operating and labor costs, and this obligation was eventually assumed by Conrail.

The drawbridge was sited in the middle of a 590 ft. wooden pile trestle. Though the technology of the bridge remained rooted in the 19th century, various improvements were effected through the years to keep the bridge in sound condition. All three sets of girders were replaced in 1917. A new tower was constructed in 1933. The B&A girders were replaced again in 1956 and, although out of service, were still in place when the bridge closed in 1989. The B&M's western track and girders were removed in 1972 following a serious marine collision, leaving the B&M with single track operation. The B&A track was taken out of service in the 1980s, after which all traffic over the bridge used the single remaining B&M track.

Prior to opening the bridge for marine passage, the bridge tender turned the block signals to red on either end, then lowered the safety gates (visible in the distance). This action severed an electrical connection with local control towers, indicating an open bridge. The bridge tender was then free to start the motors to open the bridge. Marine traffic under Draw 7 earlier in this century consisted mostly of barges serving fuel depots, while in later years traffic was primarily recreational boats. Its long, successful operation was a salute to its sound technology.

From B&M Employee Timetable No. 28, September 24, 1939: "Draw No. 7 is protected by semi-automatic color light dwarf interlocking signals, also by gates on each side of Draw, displaying target board by day and red light by night over each track. Also by red flags by day and red lights by night placed between rails of each track on each side of Draw. At night a green light in Draw Tower indicates Draw closed." Preston Johnson remembers "there were holes in the ties so that a double staff red flag had a place to stand on each side of Draw 7. Quite an operation to open and close the bridge."

Wayne D. Hills photographed the bridge on Monday, June 30, 1975. B&M RDC-1 6122 is westbound, just a few minutes before its North Station arrival.

Below: *A souvenir ticket from The Railroad Enthusiasts' Grand Junction excursion on Sunday, May 21, 1939. Preston Johnson collection.*

Boston: The Road's Anchor

Above: *This ambitious crossing shanty stood at the junction of the B&A and Massachusetts Avenue in Cambridge. The Metropolitan Storage Warehouse is the large brick building, and we are looking to the southeast, with East Boston to the left and Beacon Park to the right. The operator controlled the traffic signals at the crossing to keep the switchers working the local spurs from activating the signals when not necessary. In addition to controlling the crossing, the shanty may have been the holding point for B&A freights bound for East Boston, until they were sure they had clearance to cross the B&M's Fitchburg Division in Somerville. The railroad worked hard to keep vehicle crossings from being blocked any more than necessary. Here it's 9:27 on a humid July morning in 1961. Today only a driveway marks the spot. RWJ photo.*

72 Boston & Albany

Right: Behind MBTA Terminal Switcher 1015 is California Oil, one of the last active consignees on the branch (since moved to Salem). The date is Thursday, March 12, 1992, and the locomotive is moving light to Southhampton Street. We are at Waverly and Henry Streets in Cambridge, and in the remnants of sidings on either side of the right-of-way is ample evidence of a past, active industry. The track in the foreground is used to store excess piggyback flatcars when conditions are tight at the Beacon Park intermodal yard. David Santos photo.

Below and below left: We do not know why No. 43, a U2j class 0-8-0 built by Lima in 1918, has made such a mess of the Grand Junction Branch at the Cottage Farm Bridge this day in 1937, but we have Boston Herald photographer Leslie Jones to thank for making these two fine photographs. The white square in the upper left corner of the photo below is the result of a damaged negative. Courtesy of the Boston Public Library, Print Department.

Boston: The Road's Anchor

REMEMBERING THE GRAND JUNCTION

PRESTON JOHNSON

One of the more interesting aspects of the Grand Junction was the oil trains. Esso had a tremendous business during the war. The tankers were being sunk off the coast, so of course the oil came by rail. They needed a lot of oil in Maine at Casco Bay for refueling the Navy's ships. Casco Bay was deep enough, and could accommodate the Navy's ships. We hauled a lot of oil on the B&M plus a lot going to Esso on the B&A. We tried to keep them as solid oil trains, so they'd come out of Mechanicville with only 60-some cars, since oil was so heavy. Instead of coming in on the B&M's freight cut-off, they'd come in on the mainline by Tower H and head right into the B&A behind one of our 4000 Berkshires or 4100 Mountains over to Tower C. Then we'd have a switcher get behind them, near what we called the paint shop, and he'd pluck off the tail end and pull it back so he could put that section on the B&A. So we'd wind up with maybe 35 cars on one track and 30 cars on another. Then the switcher would take the buggy up to the hump and put it on the buggy track. The B&A would have a crew come over, and some of this stuff would have to be switched—I suppose because of the different grades of oil. While they were switching they had the B&M pretty well sewn up in that little jig-saw in front of L&F Junction (meaning Lowell and Fitchburg, from the early days when the Boston & Lowell and the Fitchburg Railroads had a junction here). It was nice working Tower H then with these oil trains, because otherwise we never handled any inbound freights.

When the B&A and the B&M interchanged cars, the railroad originating the cars took them to the other. If the B&A had cars for the B&M, usually they pulled them into Yard 9, then after pulling ahead, the engine backed to the B&A. When they had as few as four or five cars, they could back the train in so the engine would stay on the B&A end. When the B&M delivered, they hauled the cars over to Tower H and shoved them off onto the B&A.

Sometimes the B&A would switch cars out at L&F Junction—just a stone's throw east from Tower H—before taking the rest up to Yard 9. You had to be on good terms with the B&A operator at L&F. Right in the middle of our B&M interlocking were hand switches controlled by the B&A—real old, complete with switch lights. At night we could see the switch lights and could tell if we didn't have the iron. If their man wasn't in his shanty, or if he took the way bills over to the B&M yard office, and he left those switches wrong, we were not in good shape. To live up to his rules, he could have left the switch for the B&A, and locked it with their lock. Then we'd be paralyzed. We could still run the "long way," up the lead up to the paint shop and run out the Fitchburg main line with 40 cars and shove them back across the road into Yard 14. But with the busy B&M passenger train schedule, we didn't want 40 cars sitting there. Say a B&A freight was taking off, and bad weather made walking on the ground rough, so the B&A operator might jump on the buggy and ride over with the bills. If he wanted to ride the buggy over to Yard 9, where there was a pneumatic tube to get the bills up to the hump, that meant he left the switch lined wrong. The tracks between Towers H and C only held about 40 cars. Once in a while the B&A would get ambitious when they made those trains up at Beacon Park, and they would take more. Then the train would foul the Tower H interlocking until Tower C could take him.

The B&A had three regular freights from Beacon Park onto the Grand Junction: the Fast Freight in the morning; the Coke Job; and the Night Freight (which sometimes made two trips). Often they had 45-50 cars, and they never cleared everything. No matter where they stopped they blocked somebody, because the space was so tight. The B&A had a sidetrack into the Boston Elevated Railway as well in Everett.

There were no signals on the B&A Grand Junction Branch, except for B&M signals at Towers H and C. There were no signals on the B&A track on Draw 7 either—they just put the gates down and the red flags and lanterns up when they opened it.

A nasty wreck happened on the Grand Junction on Thursday, October 7, 1943. B&A Night Extra west, with engine No. 56, standing at R-28 signal at Tower C, was struck by Extra 1209 west, derailing the caboose and two cars. The cars blocked both tracks of the B&M Eastern Route. B&M trains 2546, 256, 263, 2549, and 269 were held up, as was the *Chelsea Goat*. Train 265—the last train to Portland—went out via the Western Route. The conductor on the Extra was John Maloney, an ex-wrestler, who saved his flagman's life by carrying him out of the burning caboose.

Whenever B&A trains moved east on the Grand Junction from Beacon Park, they had to hold at a certain crossing in Cambridge for clearance, so as not to block all the grade crossings. But whenever Tower H said "let them come," they had to move. Otherwise you'd have Cambridge streets tied up forever if you stopped the train.

The Railroad Enthusiasts took two trips on the Grand Junction in the 1930s. The first was May 3, 1936; the second was May 21, 1939. I rode the latter; the fare was 75¢. On both trips, the trains departed South Station mid-day and traveled over the Highland Branch to Riverside. There the trains headed east on the mainline as far as Beacon Park where the groups paused to tour the roundhouse. From there they covered the entire Grand Junction Branch, passing through industrial sections of Cambridge, Somerville, Everett, and Chelsea, all the way to the East Boston Pier. On the first trip the group was scheduled to tour the American Merchant Line steamship "American Farmer" at Pier 4, but it was delayed in New York by fog. We were luckier in 1939, and actually got to tour a ship. But here's what's so unbelievable: both trains were pulled by Tank engine No. 402, both carried coaches Nos. 488, 476, and 539, and both had 100 passengers. Railfan groups were catered to in those days! [No. 402 was also used on the Ware River excursion of November 11, 1938, following the repair of flood and hurricane damage, ed.]

There used to be a conductor on the B&A who wore women's silk panties. The story is that, onetime, going to Springfield, he got caught short and had to send his flagman into town for some fresh underpants. As a joke, the man

Lawrence *Eagle-Tribune*, February 28, 1955

Chelsea Creek Blocked

"CHELSEA, Feb. 28 (AP) — The counterweight fell from a railroad drawbridge into Chelsea Creek today, allowing the draw to fall athwart the creek in twisted condition.

"The creek was effectively blocked, isolating two tankers and blocking access to oil farms in Chelsea and Revere. No other traffic was affected.

"Boston & Albany officials, who estimated weight of the counterbalance at 'about 900 tons,' said they would use another spur track if necessary.

"However, the span itself was in such twisted condition doubt was expressed it could be repaired and might have to be demolished.

"Demolition of the span in favor of a longer bridge, to permit passage of wider tankers, has been recommended by the Boston Port development authority and the U. S. Army.

"This was the wreckage after a counterweight estimated to weigh 900 tons fell from a railroad bridge spanning Chelsea Creek in Chelsea Monday. The wreckage blocked the creek and bottled up oil tankers unloading further upstream."
(Eagle-Tribune AP Wirephoto)

Newspaper clipping from the Preston Johnson collection.

brought back women's and the conductor liked them so well he always wore them after that. In the hot weather he'd be out there switching with no shirt on, no pants on, just those panties, out there at L&F Junction. He sure was a sight with those heavy work shoes and bloomers.

Monday night we'd have sometimes a dozen cars of livestock coming out of Burnham Junction, Maine, going over to the abattoir in Brighton on the B&A. That stock was delivered to the B&A and they'd have an engine right there ready to take that livestock over. You never see livestock now. It had to be unloaded, fed, and watered every so many hours. And they had a 36-hour limit to do the job, or there would be a fine. Our chief in Greenfield would get a hold of our yardmaster and say "You've got some short-time stock coming, will you watch that?" The yardmaster would say, "Yeah, sure. If we don't have time to set it with an engine, we'll set it with a pencil." So this was how they beat the fine.

We had some unusual movements at Tower H. Sometimes you'd have private cars. Some bigshot, maybe a private industrial executive, might be traveling by private car. If he was going to Maine, say, the B&A would bring the car over with a switcher and we'd take it into the North Station, put it on a passenger train going to Portland or wherever. Then we had a character who used to work third trick yardmaster at Tower 5. (It was located on stilts just north of the High Line [New Hampshire main] bridge, and the yardmaster there controlled the snap switches at the lower ends of both Yards 8 and 9.) Since he knew a lot of the fellas, sometimes he'd take a little liberty there, and if he knew the crew and wanted a little favor done, like taking a shop car off a B&M train, he would have the B&A reach in and take the car off for him, which of course was absolutely unbelievable. Although onetime I used the B&A like that, too. No. 332, the *Ambassador* from Montreal, came in with about 12 cars and a P-3 for an engine. They used to turn it on the wye and go up over 9, to get to the yard track bridge on a very steep grade. This time they stalled, and their tail end was just clear of L&F Junction. I got ahold of the B&A guy there and said "Would you mind hooking on the tail end and shoving this guy up over the top?" So they did, and No. 332 had a B&M P-3 pulling on the head end and a B&A switcher shoving on the tail end to get him up over. The reason for the train going up on top of the receiving tracks was so they could back into yard 4 where they stored the train and serviced it. The next day a switcher would take it to the North Station for departure.

I worked at Tower H maybe three years. I liked it there; it was a railfan's paradise. There wasn't much on the B&M that didn't go past Tower H—maybe only the 4-4-0s, which were mostly on the Eastern Route. The B&A used mostly 0-8-0 switchers there, though once in a while you'd have an 0-6-0 switcher. The Coke Job always ran with either a Consolidation or a Mike. The 1200s would come over quite often.

During World War II, L&F Junction was a very busy spot. The B&A had an operator, a clerk, a yardmaster, and a car-knocker working right through all three tricks. In my diary I see that on Monday, February 16, 1942, the B&A had a field day—28 trains in 24 hours. Probably there was ship in port for which they might have had eight or nine troop trains. In those days the big passenger ships, like the Cunard-White Star Lines, used the East Boston Pier. They had hospital ships, too, to bring the wounded back. One time we had 185 cars of potatoes stored in Yard 15 because the ship coming to pick them up was torpedoed.

The Grand Junction Branch was very important to the B&A. There was a lot of very profitable business there, and they made the best of it.

III

OUTBOUND TO FRAMINGHAM

The Commuter District

On the station platform there are always two or three wooden packing-boxes, apparently marked for travel, but they are sacred from disturbance and remain on the platform forever; possibly the right train never comes along.

Booth Tarkington
THE GENTLEMAN FROM INDIANA (1899)

Boston & Albany track between Boston and Framingham was the busiest on the railroad. The main line itself was triple-tracked to Huntington Avenue (mp 1.48) then quadruple-tracked from there to .22 miles east of the Framingham station (which was at mp 21.43). Local and express trains were thus permitted to operate in the same corridor with complete autonomy and efficiency. Also there were five branch lines diverging from the main line in this same section, three of them carrying commuter train service well into the 1950s: the Highland, Newton Lower Falls, and Milford Branches. The Grand Junction Branch to East Boston was a virtual gold mine in freight revenue for the B&A right up through the 1950s. The short Saxonville Branch lost its passenger service in 1936 but generated freight revenues long after.

In this chapter we offer individual essays and photo portfolios about each of these fascinating branches, as well as significant photography of the main line operation. We were fortunate in finding an interesting mix of steam and diesel photography on the main line, especially considering that the B&A was virtually dieselized by 1951 when color film was still new to many.

In the late 1950s the Highland Branch lost all but two of its station buildings when the line was converted to trolley operation by the Metropolitan Transit Authority. Similarly the building of the Massachusetts Turnpike extension into Boston between 1962 and 1965 radically altered the look of the B&A main line from Riverside east. Four tracks were reduced to two and seven stations (leaving only Allston) were torn down, destroying a fine architectural legacy. The construction and its aftermath are graphically apparent in several of the photographs.

Especially tragic in these two projects was the loss of eight stations designed by the great Henry Hobson Richardson or his successor firm, Shepley, Rutan and Coolidge. Their joint creations caught the eye of the American architectural fraternity. And still more depots followed, the work of other architects mimicking the wonderfully squat and massive edifices which Richardson introduced (see Volume II, "Magnificent Stations," for more about the Richardson designs).

Of special note in this chapter are three curiosities: the *Train of Tomorrow*, which introduced the dome car to America; the Framingham freight house with its piquant architecture; and the campaign train of presidential candidate Thomas E. Dewey in his attempt to wrest the White House from Harry S. Truman.

Train 46, the Boston Special, ran daily from Chicago to Boston. In addition to a diner serving all meals, a sleeper, and a lounge-sleeper from the Windy City, it also added sleepers en route from Buffalo, Toronto, and Rochester. In Massachusetts it stopped in Pittsfield, Westfield, Springfield, Worcester, and Newtonville (to drop eastbound passengers) before its 9:10 a.m. arrival in Bean Town. Earlier it was named the Western Express. The train was captured just pulling out of Newtonville on a brilliantly blue Thursday, December 20, 1945 behind a J-2c Hudson. F. Rodney Dirkes photo/RWJ collection.

78 Boston & Albany

Left: *A westbound freight is just passing the Allston depot, at right, on a beautiful Sunday, February 9, 1964. The five-unit diesel set has four different locomotive types: Nos. 1633 (F-3A), 2434 (F-7B), 6006 (GP-9), 5017 (C-Liner), and 2462 (F-7B). Norton D. Clark collection.*

Below left: *At Cambridge Street, at the west end of Beacon Park Yard, NYC No. 9670 (Alco-GE 1,000 hp S-4 built in February 1952, originally numbered 8597) is being lifted back onto the iron by Crane No. X-29, after a derailment. In the background, the new Boston extension of the Massachusetts Turnpike is very much in evidence. Photographed Saturday, September 10, 1966 by George W. Turnbull.*

Right: *B&A Extra 1454 west is charging through Allston in the early morning light of Saturday, November 24, 1945. No. 1454 was the last of the B&A Berkshires to be built—by Lima in 1930. She was transferred off the B&A in January 1949.*

Below: *Later the same day, at 11:31 a.m. according to the timetable, the Knickerbocker passes through Allston en route to Chicago behind a J-2 Hudson with an RPO, express car, coaches, a diner, and sleeping cars. These two photos are remarkable for their clarity, given the ASA 10 speed of Kodachrome then. Both photos by F. Rodney Dirkes/RWJ collection.*

Above: Wednesday, January 3, 1960 was a cold, blustery day in greater Boston. This striking scene along the Charles River near Faneuil station, on the B&A six miles from South Station, is a fine portrait of how well the railroad fit into the landscape. The Massachusetts Turnpike extension would ruin this tranquility forever in just a few short years. The two-car train being pulled by NYC RS-3 No. 8260 is probably the inbound local from Worcester. Norton D. Clark photo. **Upper right:** On Saturday, September 17, 1949, NYC K-Class 4-6-2 Pacific No. 4803 has stopped at Brighton station for revenue passengers with a local train; expresses did not stop here. John Morrison photo/Ralph L. Phillips collection. **Center right:** Train 553, shown at Brighton on Tuesday, January 1, 1946, with a J-2 Hudson, is a Boston-New York Express with at least one New Haven car in its consist,

typical of this operation since its inception. **Right:** *The New England Wolverine, bringing sleepers to Boston from Cincinnati, Cleveland, Detroit, and St. Louis, along with complete dining service and reclining-seat coaches, is at Brighton two days before Christmas on Sunday, December 23, 1945. The textural quality of the J-2 Hudson's smoke against the clear sky is especially rich. Two photos by F. Rodney Dirkes/RWJ collection.*

Above left: Newton station is one of many popularly thought to be designed by H. H. Richardson, yet it was not. Still, it qualifies as being "Richardsonian," so close is the style. The building certainly has a regal quality. NYC RS-3 No. 8299 is inbound with a morning local on Saturday, March 12, 1960. The depot and two of these four main line tracks would survive only two more years.

Left: A few minutes later the New England States passed the same location (the photographer moved across a bridge) with two E-8s on its last leg into Boston. The Turnpike would be created on land to the right of the tracks. Two photos by Ben Perry.

Above: Here we see just how dramatic a change was effected in this area by the Turnpike construction. This location is Lewis Terrace, Newton, and the New England States is inbound from Chicago on Tuesday, June 11, 1963, behind an E-8 and two E-7s.

Right: E-8 No. 4044 with a Framingham-Boston local stops at Newtonville on Monday, April 16, 1962. Note how careful passengers had to be of the narrow platform and crossing the outside track. A similar condition exists today at Newtonville, West Newton, and Auburndale, where only track 2 has a platform. Passengers using Track 1 must board via narrow wooden crosswalks, very hazardous when vestibules are not spotted exactly. Two photos by Norton D. Clark.

Outbound to Framingham 83

Above: B&A Hudson No. 616 (built by Lima in 1931) has a Worcester-bound train at West Newton in September 1949. Stanley Smith photo/Norton D. Clark collection. **Below:** West Newton's grand brick depot was altered for the 1895-1897 grade-separation project, thus the odd design of the canopy. NYC RS-3 No. 8297 has an inbound morning local on Saturday, March 12, 1960. Ben Perry photo. **Opposite above:** This Tuesday, April 15, 1969 view of Train 427 at Auburndale illustrates how completely the Massachusetts turnpike extension affected the area. George W. Turnbull photo. **Opposite center:** A commuter train sweeps up the loose snow on a bright Wednesday, February 8, 1967, heading into Riverside behind RS-3 No. 5529 (originally numbered 8289 until 1966). **Opposite below:** A friendly engineer gives a big wave to the photographer on August 19, 1964 at Riverside. The train, behind RS-3 No. 8230, is running outbound on an inbound express track. Two photos by Norton D. Clark.

Above: *This strip ticket form was used to sell transportation from any B&A station to Framingham, then located on the Old Colony line to Fitchburg. In this case, the bottom stub has been stamped with "Boston C." Today's Framingham was then called South Framingham. RWJ collection.*

Outbound to Framingham

Top left: B&A Tank Engine No. 317 (Schenectady 1907) is poised at Riverside to continue its loop run onto the main line and into Boston in the late 1940s. Leon Onofri collection. **Center left:** NYC commuter coach No. 904 pauses with its train at Riverside on April 11, 1962. A trainman watches for late arrivals. In the distance can be seen both Route 128 and the original beginning of the Massachusetts Turnpike. Norton D. Clark photo. **Left:** The afternoon train for Newton Lower Falls has crossed from an express track to the Highland Branch at Riverside Station. Note the underground pas-

sageway for pedestrians at right, and the dwarf semaphore at left. The locomotive is NYC RS-3 No. 8248. Riverside was a longtime colorful scene of railroad operation. William T. Cynes photo. **Above:** This handsome portrait of Riverside was made in April 1961 by Fred Matthews. Both the station and Tower No. 16 are boarded up, and the eleven-car train is the result of reductions in train frequencies, yielding fewer passenger choices. **Right:** The Riverside dater-die stamp from April 5, 1941 has an interesting heritage: New York Central & Hudson River Railroad. RWJ collection.

Above: Wellesley Farms depot was built in 1894 at a cost of $6,516, the last from the firm of Shepley, Rutan & Coolidge. It is the only surviving Richardsonian depot with landscaping approaching the original design. When built it included a long platform canopy and was thus more impressive. On this gray Wednesday, November 27, 1968, it just looks forlorn. A two-car commuter train is inbound behind RS-3 No. 5530 (renumbered from 8291 in 1966). **Below:** It appears that this nice Dad has pulled the car over so that his two children might get to see the train more closely. Fairbanks-Morse C-Liners Nos. 5008 and 5006 have a freight at Wellesley Hills in 1954. Two photos by Norton D. Clark.

Above: Amtrak's *Bay State* is outbound at Wellesley on a bleak Wednesday, February 19, 1975. Light meals and beverages were served on this two-Budd RDC train, which ran via the B&A from Boston to Springfield, then to New Haven where it connected with the *Southern Crescent*. Norton D. Clark photo/Leon Onofri collection. *Left:* Commuter service to Marlboro via the B&A and the Old Colony began in 1870 and ended in 1937. This is a stub portion of a first class, Wellesley to Marlboro ticket. RWJ collection. *Below:* On April 23, 1977 this tattered equipment is at Natick: Penn Central GP-9 No. 7555 and three Pennsy coaches. The Boston & Maine has just begun operating south-side trains under contract to the MBTA. Richard B. Gassett photo/Leon Onofri collection.

Outbound to Framingham

Above left: B&A K-14g Pacific No. 581 (Schenectady 1913) is westbound at Weston with a local train in 1941. Norton D. Clark collection.

Left: Penn Central U-25B No. 2679 and U-33B No. 2970 pull a westbound freight though Weston on Sunday, February 20, 1972. This location, a favorite among photographers, used to sport a four-track main line and a picturesque signal bridge. Norton D. Clark photo/George W. Turnbull collection.

Above: As NYC E-8 No. 4062 brings the Framingham train through Weston on Tuesday, May 7, 1963, note how the second track over simply ends just in front of the first coach. Norton D. Clark collection.

Right: Shiny Penn-Central E-8 No. 4047 is at Weston on Tuesday, June 10, 1969 with the New England States in a sadly curtailed consist. The fourth car has a PC green window band and the fifth car is a Slumbercoach. George W. Turnbull photo.

Outbound to Framingham 91

Above: B&A KM Pacific No. 560 has arrived at Framingham c. 1948 with a local train. The locomotive is a 1913 product of Schenectady. *Below:* B&A 0-6-0 Switcher No. 149 shunts a string of cars at Framingham c. 1948. The metal rods at the lower right were used by the tower to move switch points, signals, and de-rail devices. *Opposite above:* The B&A Engine House at Framingham was located perpendicular to the freight house, visible in the distance at the left. No. 587, seen in the engine house, was a Pacific built by Schenectady in 1913. The loco at right is B&A No. 507. *Opposite below:* This photo was taken just minutes after that *below* and shows an outbound freight highballing through town behind a B&A A-1c Berkshire. A passenger train idles in the station. Note the rods from the tower controlling the dwarf semaphore. Four photos by Stanley H. Smith. The first three are from the Norton D. Clark collection; the fourth is from the E. James Gibbons collection.

Outbound to Framingham 93

Below: The B&A freight house at Framingham was a unique design. It dates from the early days of the Boston & Worcester, and its architectural heritage shows a strong Dutch influence. Note the prominent "safety" sign at the far right, reinforcing a theme emphasized by railroad managements from the very beginning. Richard Sanborn photo from May 1965.

Left: *It is Monday, November 1, 1948, and the* Train of Tomorrow *is on display at Framingham. The General Motors train included four "Astra Dome" cars (chair car, diner, all-bedroom sleeper, and round-end observation) built by Pullman to GM designs. The idea for a dome originated in 1944 when a team of GM officials rode in a diesel cab and wondered how to give the same glorious view to the public. This diesel was a 2,000 hp E-7. After national touring, the train was bought by the Union Pacific.*

Right and below: *Govenor Thomas E. Dewey paid a campaign visit to Framingham on Sunday, October 10, 1948. Speaking to the huge crowd from the observation platform, he is joined by Mrs. Dewey, Henry Cabot Lodge (to the left of Dewey), and Leverett Saltonstall (to the left of Mrs. Dewey). Newspaper headlines to the contrary, he lost. Three photos by Stanley H. Smith from the E. James Gibbons collection.*

Above: The New England States *is eastbound at Framingham behind NYC L-3a Mohawk No. 3007 on Friday, April 19, 1946. John Morrison photo/Ralph L. Phillips collection.* **Below:** *An excursion of* The Railroad Enthusiasts, Inc., *paused at Framingham on Sunday, April 27, 1958, in time for its membership to photograph the westbound* New England States *behind two E-8s, with No. 4081 in the lead. The excursionists' Budd Car train is out of sight behind the depot. Ben Perry photo.* **Right:** *A long B&A freight snakes along the beautiful Metropolitan District Commission Framingham Reservoir No. 2 at the Framingham-Ashland line in August 1967. We are looking southwest; the town line is just above the road crossing the reservoir. Aerial photographer unknown/Robert A. Buck collection.*

HIGHLAND BRANCH

The gravel hills of Needham (one as high as fifty feet, and twelve acres round) fell in the city's greedy, and familiar, press for space. What matter how far away the source of gravel in this industrial age? The twin gods of power—steam and rail—eased transportation and excavation. Victorian technology served the era's grandiose appetites. How Asa Sheldon with his plodding cart or Harry Otis with his dogged carts would have envied the modern Victorian pace! How they would have gawked at the 145 dirt cars powered by steam that traveled back and forth from Needham at forty-five minute intervals to ready the new land.

Jane Holtz Kay
Lost Boston (1980)

The Highland Branch was opened in April 1848 from Brookline Junction to Brookline Village by the Boston & Worcester which called it the Brookline Branch. Passenger service began with seven round-trips between Boston and Brookline. In May 1849 the Charles River Branch Railroad was chartered to extend the line. It opened to Newton Upper Falls in November 1852 and to Needham Center in June 1853. For about seven years, beginning in June 1858, significant revenue was derived from hauling stone and gravel from Needham to Boston for filling marshlands, creating Back Bay. Some two decades later, ice was brought by rail from Wiswall's Pond (now Crystal Lake) in Newton. For a time these rails figured importantly in the grand schemes of the New York & Boston, but such plans ended in 1867 when a parallel route through Franklin was favored instead. The Boston & Albany bought the Highland route in February 1883 as far as Cook Street, Newton Highlands for $411,400.

The B&A rebuilt and double-tracked the line, and extended it three miles northwest to its main line at Riverside, from where it began circuit trains on May 16, 1886. Trains would run from Boston to Riverside via the Highland Branch, then return on the mainline, while comparable trains ran the other way. The circuit operations were very successful and were also tried, in cooperation with the New Haven, on a Needham circuit via West Roxbury and Newton Highlands (also probably successful), and on a Milford circuit via Franklin and Ashland

98 Boston & Albany

Below Left: *No. 400—one of the celebrated B&A Class D-1a 4-6-6T Tank Engines—is outbound with three turtle-back coaches just west of Eliot in June 1948. David C. Bartlett photo.*

Right: *A two-car train of NYC Beeliners enters the main line at Brookline Junction from the Highland Branch on Sunday, April 27, 1958, with a group of rail enthusiasts. While the junction is gone today, the MBTA Green Line emerges from a tunnel about a quarter mile up the branch. The buildings at right have been replaced by the Massachusetts Turnpike. Ben Perry photo.*

Below: *Longwood was the first stop on the branch, at 3.16 miles from South Station. A single passenger boards this morning train, with RS-3 No. 8200 on the point, three weeks prior to the end of service. Allan H. Wiswall photo.*

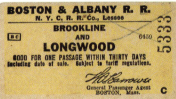

Left: *This Brookline-to-Longwood ticket represented a mere .67 mile ride. RWJ collection.*

(only modestly patronized). These joint operations of the two railroads ran afoul of Federal anti-trust rules, and the trains were discontinued April 10, 1914.

Highland Branch stations were all located on the north side of the tracks. Grade separation projects resulted in the depression of tracks through Newton Highlands and Newton Centre between 1905 and 1907.

One annotated timetable in the author's collection shows that, for a trolley strike from July 17-23, 1919, the railroad added 13 inbound (six beginning at Riverside, one at Reservoir, and six at Brookline) and six outbound week-day trains to a schedule already having 21 inbounds and 22 outbounds. Similar additions were effected on the mainline locals as well. In the busy commuting hours this resulted in trains running on headways as close as two minutes apart. Thus could a railroad rise to a public need!

Freight business was once plentiful on the Highland Branch. As early as 1890 the railroad had a gravel mining operation with several sidings on the south side of the present Woodland station site, probably ending by 1917. That year a Texaco station on B&A property was receiving gasoline there. A 1942 map shows several other sidings: Veno Lumber at Cook Street; west of Reservoir Station the Chestnut Hill water pumping stations of the Metropolitan District Commission received coal and shipped out ashes; at Brookline Village the Brookline Coal Co. and a small industrial plant were served on the south side; on the north side the town highway department received construction materials; between Park Drive and Longwood, the Longwood garage had a siding, probably for gasoline tank cars. Between Park Drive and Brookline Junction several major companies maintained warehouses: Sears Roebuck, S. S. Pierce (food purveyor), Goodyear Tire and Rubber, and Firestone Tire. Some were even served after the trolley conversion, since the railroad kept that segment, and Sears received cars until the early 1980s. The

Left: *An early morning group of commuters awaits the Boston train at Brookline station on Friday, July 19, 1957. The train is just peeking around the curve at the far left. This was the site of a freight yard. Ben Perry photo.*

Below left: *An outbound afternoon train with Alco RS-3 No. 8304 and three coaches passes Beaconsfield station on the last day, Saturday, May 31, 1958. Originally this was a private stop for the adjacent Hotel Beaconsfield, opened by the hotel c. 1907. It was built by Henry M. Whitney, the real estate developer who built and electrified the Beacon Street Trolley line in 1889, now America's oldest electric transit line. Alan H. Wiswall photo.*

Below: *The bay window of the Beaconsfield station, with its sign of raised gold lettering common on B&A stations, is also shown on the last day. Ben Perry photo.*

Luther Paul Company was a distributor for New England Coke in Newton Centre. At one time a freight house complex served the opposite side of the tracks. Jordan Marsh Co. (department store) established a warehouse at Grove Street in the early 1950s. Riverside Sand & Gravel used rail as well.

Passenger service on the Highland Branch, from an all-time peak of 30 trains in 1912, was reduced to five inbound and seven outbound trains by the last run on Saturday, May 31, 1958. The Commonwealth of Massachusetts had long contemplated placing PCC cars on the branch to connect with the downtown subway at Park Drive, and it took just 13 months to make the conversion. The new trolley operation began July 4, 1959. Ridership has remained high ever since. Of interest were plans in 1945 to have a Y-shaped route splitting beyond Newton Highlands and continuing to Needham Junction via the New Haven. It was then proposed that freight service would continue along with the conversion to trolleys. That indeed would have been an interesting operation.

Top: *Passengers disembark from an early evening commuter local at Reservoir Station on Monday, June 17, 1957. The pointed roof peak is a unique touch. Ben Perry photo.*

Above: *A year later, Sunday, August 31, 1958, three months after the last B&A train, new concrete foundation work is underway at Reservoir for the conversion to electric trolley operation. Behind the depot is the Cleveland Circle Yard of the MTA, filled with PCC cars.*

Right: *The first day of the new operation of the Highland Branch by the MTA, Saturday, July 4, 1959, with PCC Car No. 3278 at the new Reservoir Station. Two photos by Richard Jay Solomon.*

Outbound to Framingham 101

Left: *Chestnut Hill station was the third of nine stations designed by Henry Hobson Richardson for the B&A; it was completed in 1884 at a cost of $15,000. The commuter train is outbound with RS-3 No. 8224 on Thursday, October 11, 1956. This photograph has been restored by computer from an Ektachrome transparency turned red. Stanley W. Cook photo.*

Right and below: *These two photos from the Norton D. Clark collection show two aspects of Newton Centre. Budd RDC M-457 is sufficient to handle this train's business, probably in 1953 when RDCs were briefly assigned to service on the Highland Branch. Luther Paul Co.—a distributor for New England Coke—was one of just a few freight operations on the branch when its own rail service ended in 1958.*

102   Boston & Albany

Right: Newton Highlands station was completed in 1887 at a cost of $12,578, the first of 23 stations designed by Shepley, Rutan and Coolidge, successors to Henry Hobson Richardson. The unusual double roof design resulted when the building was significantly altered for a track depression project between 1905 and 1907. The lower story was created by adding a façade to the foundation walls and included only one small room. The station still stands along the MBTA's Green Line; it has served as an auto parts store for more than 35 years. This photo by Ben Perry was made on Saturday, July 20, 1957.

Below: Thirty-six years later, on Friday, December 31, 1993, MBTA No. 3484, an LRV built by Boeing-Vertol, is outbound at the same location on the Green Line in the early morning snow. Brian Solomon photo.

Outbound to Framingham   103

Above: Two NYC Beeliners, Nos. M-452 and M-461, carried an excursion of The Railroad Enthusiasts, Inc., over the Highland Branch on Sunday, April 27, 1958. It also covered the Milford and Saxonville branches. This location was called Cook Street in the employee timetable. The branch to the left is New Haven trackage from Needham and was the original route completed to Needham Center in June 1853. The B&A created its circuit operation in 1886 by building from here three miles to Riverside. **Below:** At Newton Highlands the B&A crossed over the busy Route 9 to Worcester. RS-3 No. 8265 (built June 1951) is pulling a Budd RDC, perhaps as a result of mechanical failure, on Friday, July 19, 1957. Two photos by Ben Perry.

104   Boston & Albany

Above: This hazy-day panorama of Woodland station was made on Saturday, July 20, 1957. At left is a golf course. Ben Perry photo.

Left and below: Eliot station as seen on Thursday, May 29, 1958 with a morning, five-car commuter train, and in 1972 with a single MBTA PCC car. Photos by (left) Lawson K. Hill and (below) Brian Solomon.

Below left: The Riverside-to-Woodland ticket was issued at Riverside on April 5, 1941. RWJ collection.

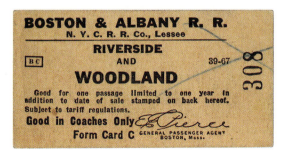

Outbound to Framingham   105

Above: An afternoon commuter train idles at Riverside after a revenue run from Boston on Wednesday, July 17, 1957. Ben Perry photo. *Above right:* This Saturday, May 10, 1958 view clearly shows the layout at Riverside. The train in the foreground will proceed to Boston on the Highland Branch, while that in the distance will go to Boston over the main line. At left is B&A Tower 15, controlling the interlocking of the four-track main line with the double-track Highland Branch, also used here by Newton Lower Falls Branch trains. Allan H. Wiswall climbed a signal mast to make the photo. *Below right:* The very last Highland Branch train heads past the Woodland golf course on Saturday, May 31, 1958. Norton D. Clark photo.

A Highland Branch conductor gazes ahead as his train arrives at one of the foliage-thick commuter stations along the branch. Norton D. Clark photo.

Outbound to Framingham 107

NEWTON LOWER FALLS BRANCH

Newton Lower Falls station is within the boundaries of the town of Wellesley. Two locomotives were housed at night at Lower Falls. One made a trip to Boston and back; the other ran the two-car connection to Riverside, and on at least one trip a day was a mixed train. On one or two other trips a coach or two was handled through to Boston on a Circuit train . . .

No. 194, the old "Westboro," renumbered 276, ended her days on the Lower Falls branch . . .

An oldish conductor (I believe named Rice) handled the Lower Falls train. As business fell off, he and the engineer (no fireman) handled the one-car train with old 276.

Lewis H. Bullard
"Memories of The Boston & Albany"
THE RAILROAD ENTHUSIAST (1941)

This 1.1-mile branch was opened January 18, 1847, when it served as the end of Boston-Newton short-turn runs. In July 1848 the railroad operated five round-trips. Upon completion of the Highland Circuit in 1886, most service to Lower Falls was provided by shuttles from Riverside. The May 28, 1899 Employee's Timetable lists 18 round-trips to Riverside, with the admonition "No trains will be run over the branch with cars ahead of the engine." It must have been very tempting on such a short branch. One early morning run had only one minute to run the engine around its coach at Riverside. Beginning on February 1, 1904* the B&A electrified the line and operated a 60 ft. interurban car (New York Central & Hudson River No. 11), soon known affectionately as the "Ping-Pong." In case of breakdown it could be replaced by steam power which was always nearby. Electric power derived from the Middlesex & Boston Street Railway, which crossed the branch at Lower Falls. In 1930 the M&B converted from trolleys to buses, and the B&A returned steam to the branch rather than invest in a power plant. Frequency of service was reduced. The "Ping-Pong" ended its days on the B&A as a service car for the signal department, numbered X2157.

In 1912, under electrification, there were still 18 daily connections at Riverside, 15 in 1919. In 1931 there were eight round-trips, four in September 1933 (three on Saturday). In 1941 there were four week-day and two Saturday round-trips. In 1951 there were four week-day round trips, but only one in April 1956. The last run was in August 1957. For most of the branch's life, timetable listings stated that "All trains stop on signal at Pine Grove."

Track between Riverside and Pine Grove was relocated in 1926 (adding .15 mile) both to avoid a bridge replacement and to relocate the track off park property. The new alignment shared the Highland Branch for a short stretch at Riverside. Trackage south of the MBTA's

*Thomas J. Humphrey, author of *Boston's Commuter Rail*, has confirmed, through contemporary newspaper accounts, that this date is correct.

Left: *Wednesday, July 17, 1957, one month before the last passenger run, NYC RS-3 No. 8249 has arrived with the evening commuter train. The little wooden shanty at the left has long since replaced the handsome 1887 stone depot. Ben Perry photo.*

Above: NYC Ticket from Trinity Place to Newton Lower Falls. William T. Clynes collection.

Right: The last passenger train on the branch, August 1957. Norton D. Clark collection.

Center right: This is the famous Ping Pong, actually New York Central & Hudson River No. 11. It was used on the branch from 1904 to 1930, when electrification was dropped. Kevin T. Farrell collection.

Below: The flagman has just hopped aboard the slow-moving NYC RS-3 No. 8258 as it crosses the street at Pine Grove with a single boxcar for the branch on Wednesday, December 11, 1963. Norton D. Clark collection.

Below right: Passengers at Pine Grove were provided with this simple but attractive shelter. Norton D. Clark collection.

Riverside yard was not used after May 30, 1972, when the last freight ran (a total of 90 carloads were handled in all of 1971). The whole branch was abandoned in 1976 when Conrail succeeded Penn Central. But in 1995 the MBTA completely rebuilt the track connection between the old Riverside Station and the MBTA Riverside yards, to allow interchange of heavy track-work equipment directly between the Green Line and the commuter rail system, instead of being trucked.

Outbound to Framingham

CROSSING THE CONTINENT

The Boston & Albany was quick to embrace the public's interest in the possibilities of air travel. Leaving Boston on Friday evening, a traveller could arrive Los Angeles the following Monday morning, saving a day and a half from an all-rail scheule. This was merely a precursor of the future competition from the airlines in the 1950s which came very close to eliminating the long-distance passenger train in America. From the B&A system timetable of November 1, 1929.

RAIL-AIR SERVICE

TO THE PACIFIC COAST

The Boston & Albany Railroad and New York Central Lines

Universal Air Lines --- Western Air Express

Tri-Motored Cabin Planes

Via Universal Air Lines System

West-bound

Southwestern Limited — Example by Days
- Lv. Boston (B.&A.R.R.) ..... 2.15 p.m. — Fri.
- Ar. Cleveland ..... 6.15 a.m. — Sat.

Universal Air Lines System
- Lv. Cleveland ..... 7.10 a.m. — Sat.
- Ar. Chicago ..... 9.05 a.m. — Sat.
- Lv. Chicago ..... 9.45 a.m. — Sat.
- Ar. Kansas City ..... 1.50 p.m. — Sat.
- Lv. Kansas City ..... 2.30 p.m. — Sat.
- Ar. Garden City ..... 5.20 p.m. — Sat.

Santa Fe Railway
- Lv. Garden City ..... 6.10 p.m. — Sat.
- Ar. Los Angeles ..... 9.15 a.m. — Mon.

East-bound

Santa Fe Railway — Example by Days
- Lv. Los Angeles ..... Daily 12.30 p.m. — Mon.
- Ar. Garden City ..... 7.53 a.m. — Wed.

Universal Air Lines System
- Lv. Garden City ..... 8.10 a.m. — Wed.
- Ar. Kansas City ..... 11.48 a.m. — Wed.
- Lv. Kansas City ..... 12.18 p.m. — Wed.
- Ar. Chicago ..... 3.53 p.m. — Wed.
- Lv. Chicago ..... 4.00 p.m. — Wed.
- Ar. Cleveland ..... 7.45 p.m. — Wed.

Southwestern Limited
- Lv. Cleveland ..... 9.00 p.m. — Wed.
- Ar. Boston (B.&A.R.R.) ..... 12.20 p.m. — Thurs.

FARES

The regular rail fares will apply between all points where train is used.

Airplane fares as follows:	One-Way	Round Trip
Cleveland and Garden City, Kansas	$127.25	$238.00
Cleveland and Chicago	37.50	70.00
Cleveland and Kansas City	83.25	155.75
Chicago and Garden City, Kansas	89.75	167.75
Chicago and Kansas City	45.75	85.50

Automobile Transportation furnished between railroad terminals and airport.

For complete information, tickets and reservations, consult any Boston & Albany ticket agent.

Via Western Air Express

West-bound

Western Express — Example by Days
- Lv. Boston (B.&A.R.R.) ..... 6.10 p.m. — Fri.
- Ar. Chicago ..... 7.30 p.m. — Sat.

Chicago & Alton
- Lv. Chicago ..... 8.00 p.m. — Sat.
- Ar. Kansas City ..... 8.00 a.m. — Sun.

or Santa Fe
- Lv. Chicago ..... 8.15 p.m. — Sat.
- Ar. Kansas City ..... 8.10 a.m. — Sun.

Western Air Express
- Lv. Kansas City ..... 8.30 a.m. — Sun.
- Ar. Los Angeles ..... 8.00 p.m. — Sun.

East-bound

Western Air Express — Example by Days
- Lv. Los Angeles ..... Daily 5.00 p.m. — Mon.
- Ar. Kansas City ..... 7.00 p.m. — Mon.

Chicago & Alton
- Lv. Kansas City ..... 8.00 p.m. — Mon.
- Ar. Chicago ..... 8.00 a.m. — Tues.

or Santa Fe
- Lv. Kansas City ..... 8.35 p.m. — Mon.
- Ar. Chicago ..... 8.10 a.m. — Tues.

or Rock Island
- Lv. Kansas City ..... 8.40 p.m. — Mon.
- Ar. Chicago ..... 9.15 a.m. — Tues.

The Wolverine
- Lv. Chicago ..... 11.00 a.m. — Tues.
- Ar. Boston ..... 10.45 a.m. — Wed.

(SCHEDULES SUBJECT TO CHANGE WITHOUT NOTICE)

BOSTON & ALBANY R. R.

EIGHT TRAINS TO THE WEST DAILY

SAXONVILLE BRANCH

The Saxonville train was hauled by No. 205, the "Saxonville," built by the B&A in 1872. George Reid was conductor, and the road gave him time off when he was elected to the Legislature. Perly Ordway was brakeman, a man of strong religious temperament who sang the names of the stations. The baggage-master was a small man who wouldn't allow cigarette smoking in the combination car.

Lewis H. Bullard
"Memories of The Boston & Albany"
THE RAILROAD ENTHUSIAST (1941)

The 3.8-mile branch to Saxonville was opened by the Boston & Worcester on July 6, 1846. A year earlier a group of citizens petitioned the Legislature to build a line linking Framingham (via Saxonville) with Weston on the Fitchburg Railroad, and it was this action which secured the B&W's promise to build from Natick to Saxonville. In addition to thwarting the Fitchburg, the B&W was banking on business from a "large manufacturing establishment," according to the 1850 Annual Report, "since destroyed by fire." The report lists a capital cost of $81,132, working expenses of $4,651, and income of $2,573. Still they kept it operating, hoping that the manufacturing company would be resurrected. There were many on-line industries over the years, most now closed. Continental Baking Co. remains on a spur south of Cochituate, receiving covered hoppers of ingredients for Wonder Bread and Hostess Twinkies.

The original passenger schedule of July 1846 listed trains leaving Boston at 8:40 a.m., 2:15 p.m., and 5:30 p.m. Trains departed Saxonville at 7:00 and 10:00 a.m., and 4:00 p.m. Subsequent to that, for many years the railroad offered two daily round-trips, and Lewis Bullard reported that the crew "ran a mixed job to Natick in the middle of the day" (see p. 26). Timetables between 1893 and 1935 show a single round-trip. Then in 1936 the B&A replaced rail service with a bus (actually a car driven by the station agent), until 1943 when all passenger service was stopped. Excursion trains occasionally made their way onto the branch after 1936, however.

Ownership of the property passed from New York Central to Penn Central to Conrail. The track north of Cochituate, 2.5 miles from the main line, was torn up about 1987, after having sat idle for many years. The MBTA has considered building a large parking lot on this spur—space in Framingham being inadequate—and terminating short-run commuter trains here. The plan has received less public attention since the reestablishment of through Boston-Worcester service in 1995. An announced sale to RailTex in 1996 was still unresolved at press time.

The New England Division of the Railroad Enthusiasts, Inc., explored the Saxonville Branch on Sunday, April 27, 1958, using NYC Beeliners M452 and M461. This was one of several excursions to travel this branch after the end of passenger service in 1936. This unnoted location was photographed somewhere along the 3.8-mile branch. It appears that the inhabitants of the nearby house have been dumping trash next to the right-of-way. Norton D. Clark collection.

MILFORD BRANCH

The villages on this branch are thrifty and growing, their people enterprising to an extraordinary degree, and their business rapidly increasing. One hundred forty houses and shops have been built during the year in the town of Milford alone. It may be confidently expected that the capital invested in this branch will in a few years yield a fair return.

1850 ANNUAL REPORT
Boston & Worcester Railroad

The Directors of the Boston & Worcester were contemplating the addition of several branches, as noted in the June 1, 1846 *Annual Report*. Among these was a line to Milford which could provide rail access to the numerous pink granite quarries between Holliston and Milford. (Indeed, Milford granite would eventually be used in B&A stations in Framingham, Southville, and Ashland, and in Albany Union Station as well. Norcross Co., who maintained a quarry in Milford, was the contractor for dozens of B&A stations.) A year later construction had started on the line to Milford and was expected to be complete before autumn. In the event, the branch opened halfway at Holliston on September 6, 1847, and was opened to Milford on July 5, 1848, 12 miles from Framingham. Permission was sought from the Legislature to build an additional eight miles to Blackstone, near Woonsocket—possibly part of a plan to reach Providence—but the Legislature denied the plan. Milford was also served later by two other railroads; the Milford & Woonsocket (later New Haven) reached the town in August 1868, while the Grafton & Upton did not arrive until May 1890. The New Haven depot was just 150 ft. west and across the street from the B&A depot.

In 1909 the B&A replaced the original 1848 station with one of granite from its own quarry, at a cost of $20,000. The same quarry also provided stone for other Milford Branch buildings, bridges, and structures, the

most picturesque being the Woodland Street Viaduct.

Beginning passenger service involved changing trains at Framingham. Two daily trains left Milford 6:40 a.m. and 4:00 p.m. Southbound runs left Framingham after the arrival of the 8:00 a.m. and 4:00 p.m. trains from Boston, and the 3:45 p.m. from Worcester. Through service from Milford to Boston began in 1886. The railroad was operating six weekday round-trips in 1899, expanded to ten in 1908; four were through trains while the other six required a change at Framingham.

Between 1911 and 1914 the New Haven Railroad operated circuit trains routed Boston-Franklin-Milford-Ashland on the New Haven's Midland Division, then via the B&A main line to Boston. Since these trains ran express over the B&A east of Ashland, travel from Milford to Boston was faster than on the B&A's own local trains, despite the longer distance. This innovative service was ended by Federal anti-trust action in 1914. New Haven passenger service to Milford ended in 1920. The five miles of New Haven track from Ashland to Hopkinton were abandoned in 1938. Track was cut back to a quarry in North Milford in 1953, then to an industrial area north of Milford station in 1959.

Seven B&A weekday round trips appeared in the November 1919 schedule, six in 1931, five in 1936, four in 1942, three in 1948, four in 1951, then just one in 1953. Until the late 1940s, about half these trains ran through while the others required changing at Framingham. Even though there were just 200 daily riders in 1954, the Massachusetts Department of Public Utilities rebuffed the B&A's petition to remove the train. But as ridership dropped to 30 by 1959, permission was granted. It was cold and snowy on Friday, March 27, 1959 when the last evening train arrived in Milford, ending 111 years of passenger service.

Freight traffic was once very lucrative. Commodities shipped in 1917 from 16 businesses on the branch included coal, grain, granite, grape juice, hay, heaters, ice, oil, shoes, and wool. But, by the mid 1960s, service was provided just tri-weekly, while by 1970 it was provided only as needed. The last train over the *entire* branch ran January 5, 1972, and in late 1974 some five miles of rail were removed from Milford to Hopping Brook. Dennison Manufacturing Co. moved from downtown Framingham to Metcalfs in the early 1970s. When their main supplier began shipping in jumbo boxcars which wouldn't fit through the Highland Street Arch, Dennison gave up on rail service altogether. In 1986 the branch was still in service to Holliston where Conrail served Axton-Cross Co., and State Lumber Co. One very large customer was the General Motors Assembly plant in Framingham which still received unfinished automobiles on tri-level freight cars, undertaking finishing work such as upholstery. Completed vehicles were then shipped out on trucks. This plant finally closed in 1990 after several temporary shutdowns. Conrail currently operates a transfer facility for finished cars directly from rail to truck in the former G. M. yard. After Axton-Cross Co. ceased using rail service in 1995, trackage south of the G. M. Plant was taken out of service; Conrail intends to abandon it.

Photo: In June 1958, NYC RS-3 No. 8346 pulls a B&A commuter train across the Woodland Street Viaduct in Holliston. Crossing Jar Brook and built of Milford pink granite, the structure was a famous landmark on the line. Norton D. Clark collection.

Above: This Milford-to-Holliston ticket was issued June 17, 1954 at Milford. The distance between stations was 6.54 miles. William T. Clynes collection.

Outbound to Framingham

Above: A two-car train of NYC Beeliners conveyed an excursion of The Railroad Enthusiasts, Inc., over the Milford Branch on Sunday, April 27, 1958, using cars M-452 and M-461. A photo stop was made at the Highland Street Arch in Milford, and a Road Foreman of Engines rode the side of the car to check for clearances, since this was the first and only occasion that Beeliners ever travelled this branch. Could it be that the railroad had forgotten about the tunnel's existence when it approved the trip? Ben Perry photo.

Below: Here are two different types of tickets used by the B&A on the Milford Branch. The Framingham to Metcalfs ticket is a standard, pre-printed ticket for a single ride. It was issued June 17, 1954—Bunker Hill day in Massachusetts. The handwritten ticket from Milford to Metcalfs was part of a longer form which agents used for long-distance tickets, often involving more than one railroad. The dark blue dater-die stamp is from the back of the same ticket, made by the Milford agent's stamping machine. William T. Clynes collection.

Below: When this photo of the East Holliston depot was made on November 2, 1952, the building was also used as a post office. Today it is a residence. Stanley W. Cook photo.

114   **Boston & Albany**

Top: *Seen from Central Street are both the B&A freight house and passenger depot on an earlier excursion on Sunday, March 10, 1957. Note from the crossbuck that one track extends across the street to the southwest to connect with the New Haven Railroad. This connection may have been established in 1938 when the New Haven closed its branch from Milford north to the B&A between Hopkinton and Ashland. The Milford depot later served as a liquor store for a time.*

Above: *The two-car train of two NYC Beeliners has arrived at Milford depot with the 1958 excursion, which also visited the Saxonville and Highland Branches. Two photos by Ben Perry.*

Above right: *A pair of old-style crossing signs, seen on October 5, 1960, at Rocky Hill in Milford, where a passenger shelter was situated until 1954. The stop was established in 1888 for workers at the Norcross Granite Quarry. Norton D. Clark collection.*

Below right: *During the photo stop at Holliston on the 1958 excursion, the fireman checks the car's underbody as the conductor and brakeman wait for the photographers to complete their shots. Today the building is a cocktail lounge. Ben Perry photo.*

Outbound to Framingham

IV
OVER THE HILL TO WORCESTER
Main Line Running

Mr. Simeon Phinney, wheezing comfortably at his musical pipe, drew an ancient silver watch from his pocket and looked at its dial. Quarter past six. Time to be getting down to the depot and the post office. At least a dozen male citizens of East Harniss were thinking that very thing at that very moment. It was a community habit of long standing to see the train come in and go after the mail. The facts that the train bore no passengers in whom you were intimately interested, and that you expected no mail made little difference. If you were a man of thirty or older, you went to the depot or the "club," just as your wife or sisters went to the sewing circle, for sociability and mild entertainment. If you were a single young man you went to the post office for the same reason that you attended prayer meeting. If you were a single young lady you went to the post office and prayer meeting to furnish a reason for the young man.

Joseph C. Lincoln
THE DEPOT MASTER (1891)

Boston & Albany's four-track main line ended just .22 miles east of the Framingham station, the west end of the commuter territory. The remaining 23 miles of track to Worcester were double-iron, except for a 2.57-mile section of triple iron between Framingham and Ashland. Between Boston and Framingham there was but a single branch: that to Millbury, opened in 1837 to access the lucrative textile industry. Also of interest is the little, 15.37-mile Grafton & Upton Railroad (photo on p. 125) which extends from the B&A main line at North Grafton (1.32 miles east of Millbury Junction) to Milford, carrying salt, flour, and miscellaneous commodities.

Worcester is the site of one of the most fascinating passenger stations on the B&A, designed by Philadelphia architects Watson and Huckel and completed by the B&A in 1911. Patronage was excellent until after World War II, but so poor by 1965 that all but a small ticket and waiting area in the old barber shop were closed. The Penn Central Corporation sold the building to a local developer. Despite its 1970 bankruptcy, Penn Central operated Boston commuter service until 1975, when daily ridership had fallen to 10 riders each way. Two decades of vandalism and weather took a heavy toll on the building. Now an energetic new group, the Union Station Alliance, is building cooperation among local forces and government agencies to restore the building as a rail-bus transportation center. The plan calls for a variety of retail and commercial spaces, making the station friendly to adjoining streets and neighborhoods, and emphasizing pedestrian traffic over vehicles. By the time the first bids were solicited in February 1997—for $19 million in initial work—some $28.5 million in federal and state funds had been committed to the total project.

The MBTA restored Worcester commuter operation in 1994 after a 19-year hiatus, beginning with rush-hour service: three morning inbound trips to Boston and three evening outbounds. A second track, removed in the early 1980s for lack of foresight, was restored in 1996 to allow commuter and Conrail trains to operate simultaneously, minimizing conflicts. Ridership has been excellent.

Train 27, the New England States, blasts out of Framingham behind NYC L-3a 4-6-2 No. 3012 on a wintry but bright Friday, March 17, 1950. This was the most deluxe of several daily Boston-Chicago runs, and it carried several sleepers and a diner. Its scheduled Boston departure was at 2:10 p.m., with arrival in Chicago the following morning at 7:50. The distinctive lines of the B&A freight house can be seen at right. Stephen R. Payne photo.

NEW YORK CITY TRAINS

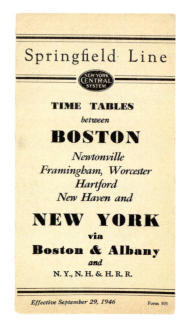

The colorful graphics of these B&A brochures advertising the Boston-New York City trains illustrate how significant this business once was. That at left was issued October 28, 1895 and listed five daily trains. The center one was issued September 26, 1926 and listed only four trains. That at right was issued September 29, 1946 and again listed five trains. RWJ collection.

We left Boston at half past two in the afternoon of March 6, 1855 by what is called the Boston and New York Express Line . . . The whole distance is 236 miles, which was accomplished in nine hours, and the fare was five dollars, a little over two cents a mile.

The train stopped 20 minutes at Springfield for an early supper. Bodily refreshment is never lost sight of in the arrangements of American traveling. Almost immediately after leaving Springfield, night fell and before long it was quite dark. The seats in the cars of this line are the least disagreeable I met with in America; the backs are sufficiently high to form an easy rest for the head and the footboard adjusts itself to give your legs repose. The result of all this, especially after supper and in the dark, which is only partially dispelled by the car lamps, is that most people fell asleep, so the last part of the journey was quiet enough.

William Ferguson
"The Baggage Agent"
AMERICA BY RIVER AND RAIL (London, 1856)

Today we travel by train between Boston and New York City on Amtrak, riding on what our generation knew as the New Haven Railroad's Shore Line. However, the very first trains serving those two cities began March 9, 1840, running via Worcester, Norwich, and *steamboats*, according to that day's Boston *Advertiser*. At first the train departed at 1:00 p.m., then later at 3:00 p.m., after the steamboat wharf connections at Norwich were completed. The earlier time allowed passengers to board the boat before dark. Fare was $5.

All-rail service via Springfield was established May 14, 1849, leaving Boston at 7:00 a.m., arriving New York at 4:00 p.m. The eastbound train ran one hour later. A second westbound train, departing Boston at 4:00 p.m., terminated at New Haven where passengers boarded an overnight steamship. Such Boston-New York railway-steamship connections remained popular long after rails made them unnecessary; the last to operate was the famous Fall River Boat Train, closing in July 1937.

Afternoon all-rail service was begun eastbound on October 8, 1849 (New York 2:00 p.m.-Boston 11:15 p.m.), and westbound on April 24, 1850 (Boston 2:30 p.m.-New York 11:30 p.m.).

The Springfield *Republican* of October 9, 1849 noted: "The new arrangement of trains commenced yesterday, and the evening train from New York had 27 passengers for Boston, for which city they left at 8:15 p.m. This line will undoubtedly prove a highly popular one, if sufficient time is allowed the passengers to get a good supper. Nothing less than half an hour will answer for this, and if the road managers desire to succeed they must see to it that the passengers have it."

The first night train to New York was the *Sunday Mail* in November 1859 (westbound, Boston 6:30 p.m.-New York 3:10 a.m., and eastbound, New York 5:00 p.m.-Boston 1:15 a.m.). The first regular night train began in November 1860 (westbound, Boston 9:00 p.m.-New York 5:50 a.m., and eastbound,

Train 559, the Boston-New York Express, is westbound at Webster Junction on Saturday, June 11, 1949. Locomotive No. 600 is the first of 20 J-2 class Hudsons built for the B&A by Alco and Lima between 1928 and 1931. The locomotive's proportions were stunning indeed. The train departed Boston daily at 3:15 p.m. and arrived Grand Central Terminal at 8:48 p.m. In this day's consist are a wooden express car, New Haven parlor car, Pullman parlor car, New Haven diner, and three New Haven "American Flyer" streamlined coaches. Power would be changed at Springfield where the train paused for 13 minutes. Lawson K. Hill photo.

New York 8:00 p.m.-Boston 6:15 a.m.) After the Shore Line night train (which originated in New London at that time) began in August 1861, it joined the above train at New Haven, arriving New York at 4:50 a.m.

The creation of the New York, New Haven & Hartford Railroad occurred in 1872, but the drawbridge spanning the Thames River was not completed until October 1889. It was only thereafter that the New Haven's Shore Line could compete successfully with the B&A/NH New York trains via Springfield.

The chart below illustrates how the schedules of the only four B&A-NH Boston-New York trains running in 1935 compare with four selected NH Shore Line trains (of which there were 15 total). Although the B&A generally operated comparable equipment, its schedules were noticeably slower despite a mere 3.5 mile-longer route via Springfield. The glamour of the New Haven's extra-fare *Yankee Clipper* and *Merchants Limited* was hard to beat, especially with the "afternoon tea served" on the *Clipper*. But for anyone living west of Boston on the B&A, these trains via Worcester, Springfield, and Hartford provided fine service indeed to New York City.

Boston to New York City trains from the July 1935 *Official Guide of the Railways* (all trains daily)

No.	Leave	Arrive	Duration	Accommodations	Train Name
Via Springfield using the BOSTON & ALBANY and NEW YORK, NEW HAVEN & HARTFORD RAILROADS					
51	9:15 a.m.	3:10 p.m.	5 hrs., 55 min.	parlor, diner	*New York Express**
53	11:00 a.m.	4:55 p.m.	5 hrs., 55 min.	parlor-buffet, diner	*Boston-New York Express**
59	3:00 p.m.	8:55 p.m.	5 hrs., 55 min.	parlor-buffet, diner	*Twilight Express**
55	11:00 p.m.	6:15 a.m.	7 hrs., 15 min.	sleepers (non-air-conditioned)**	*New York Express*
Via Providence using the NEW YORK, NEW HAVEN & HARTFORD RAILROAD (only selected trains shown)					
11	9:00 a.m.	2:15 p.m.	5 hrs., 15 min.	lounge, parlor, diner	*Bay State**
23	12:00 noon	4:30 p.m.	4 hrs., 30 min.	club, parlor, diner, observation (no baggage handled, no coaches)	*Yankee Clipper* ***
27	4:00 p.m.	8:30 p.m.	4 hrs., 30 min.	club smoking, parlor, diner, observation smoking (no coaches)	*Merchants Limited* ***
3	11:30 p.m.	5:15 a.m.	5 hrs., 45 min.	sleepers (coaches Sat. night only)	*Owl**

*air-conditioned   **Cars ready for occupancy at 9:00 p.m. in both Boston & Worcester. Vacate at 6:20 a.m.   ***Extra fare.

Over the Hill to Worcester

DINING ABOARD

On the premise, perhaps, that patrons of the Boston section of The Century were more devoted to high thinking than to haute cuisine, meals on the Boston & Albany were somewhat less [than] Lucullan. The menus for August 1933 listed a plate special for $1 that included soup, panned fresh shrimp, roast beef au jus, green apple pie and chocolate nut pudding with whipped cream, and $1.25 combinations with a choice of Cotuit oysters or vegetable soup, broiled filet of blue fish or braised chicken Creole, fig and grapefruit salad, cheese or individual strawberry shortcake. On the à la carte, Cotuit cocktail was listed at thirty cents, broiled Boston scrod, seventy cents, roast prime beef, seventy cents and fresh asparagus on toast with melted butter or Hollandaise, thirty-five cents.

Lucius Beebe
20TH CENTURY (1962)

The Boston & Albany used two distinct logo patterns on its china, called Pittsfield and Berkshire. The latter pattern is featured on these pages.
Opposite: *The waiters have almost completed laying a lunch setting aboard the 20th Century; we lack just a few pieces of silverware. Three silver items grace the rear: sugar bowl, teapot, and creamer. Ahead of these are a 10 oz. pitcher, an 11-inch celery platter, and a gravy boat. The left setting includes an 8-inch soup plate, an 8x5-inch rectangular platter, a soup cup, and a butter plate. The right setting includes a 7-inch breakfast plate, a 6-inch au gratin dish, a 5-inch baked apple dish, and a butter plate.*

Below: *A 2x6-inch gravy boat. The Berkshire pattern items are all backstamped with the initials of Jones, McDuffy & Stratton Co., Boston. The silverware was named Carlton and was manufactured by Reed & Barton. Michael J. Sullivan china and silver collection/Brian Solomon photo (table and gravy boat), Bob Millard photo (background plate).*

Above: *A Boston & Albany dining car c. 1900, with the tables immaculately set for dinner with silver and fresh linen napkins. Fruit and bread are already on the tables as a first course, and wine lists and menus tell of the fare to come. Note the round B&A logo on the menus. Photo courtesy of the Society for the Preservation of New England Antiquities.*

Left: *These two menu covers are from a 19-part series of 148 items honoring colleges and universities along New York Central routes. The Harvard cover is from the first series in July 1947, while the MIT cover is from the third series of February 1948. The actual menus were printed separately and inserted into the covers. RWJ collection.*

Over the Hill to Worcester

Top left: *Cordaville depot sits unused and probably forgotten amidst a lingering snow blanket this Sunday February 16, 1969. The building was clearly influenced in style by H. H. Richardson. Norton D. Clark photo.*

Above left: *The inside cover of a Boston-Ashland monthly commutation ticket issued March 31, 1941 to one L. Proth who, according to the punches, was a male of medium stature with a medium, smooth-faced complexion. RWJ collection.*

Left: *The late afternoon sun contrasts with threatening skies and highlights the rich MBTA paint scheme on F40 No. 1072 in August 1989. Framingham was then the western terminus of commuter operation but, in the fall of 1994, operation to Worcester was begun again with three daily round-trips. Brian Solomon photo.*

Above: *Four NYC GE U-25B locomotives convey a freight over the stone arch bridge in Ashland on Sunday, July 17, 1966. The diesels were built in December 1966 and were passed on to both the Penn Central and Conrail.*

Below: *The New England States' locomotives, E-7 No. 4021 and E-8 No. 4047, are on the ground this Tuesday, July 8, 1969, and a large crew is on hand to get traffic moving again at Ashland. Two photos by Norton D. Clark.*

Above: B&A J-2c Hudson No. 615, built by Lima in 1931, roars past a target signal on a curve at Westboro with the New England Wolverine, a daily Chicago-Boston train which traveled north of Lake Erie through Canada on the Michigan Central. At various times in its history the train also carried sleepers from Cincinnati, Cleveland, Detroit, and St. Louis. Stephen R. Payne photo. *Below:* The Southville depot was definitely copied from the H. H. Richardson designs, particularly the curved window in the roof. The pink granite came from a Milford quarry, as it did for the B&A depots in Ashland, Framingham, and Albany Union Station. Richard Sanborn photo from December 1971.

Above right: B&A H-5j class 2-8-2 No. 1206 moves through Cordaville with two freight cars and a caboose on Tuesday, November 15, 1949. Note the mail stanchion just to the right of the caboose. The local station agent would place the U. S. mail bag in the holder at the top where it would be grabbed by the hook on a passing Railway Post Office car. Stephen R. Payne photo.

Right: A NYC peddler freight led by RS-3 No. 8314 is leaving North Grafton westbound for Worcester after interchanging with the Grafton & Upton. John F. Kane photo. *Inset:* The Grafton & Upton was a very small but nonetheless beloved New England institution. Here is its GE 44-tonner No. 9 (built in July 1946) at Upton on March 6, 1972. Richard B. Gassett photo/Leon Onofri collection.

MILLBURY BRANCH

On summer mornings in the early 1960s when my brother John and sister Susan were youngsters, the Millbury local came by just about 9:00 each morning, backing from Millbury Junction with the conductor and crew standing on the buggy platform. Crossing route 22, about a half mile away, the engineer would sound the horn of the NYC RS unit. Closer to our house, the crew tooted the buggy whistle. Our back door would fly open and my brother and sister would bolt out, head down the path, and run across the little dam at the trout pond on Bonnie Brook. Then up to the old cow path leading to the tracks where the train backed across a big cinder-covered fill. The buggy crew waved to the kids and they waved back, faces beaming. But they were really waiting for the locomotive and the big friendly engineer. He looked kind of like the Santa of the 1940s Coca Cola ads, maybe a little more rugged looking, like Burl Ives, but clean shaven. He was the classic brave engineer, neat as a pin with pin-striped overalls, white gloves with large cuffs, and a white-striped engineer's hat. With a big White Owl cigar firmly clenched between his teeth he leaned out the cab window and threw the kids a package, neatly wrapped in white butcher's paper and tied with a string, filled with candy bars bought by the crew.

*William G. Dulmaine, Jr.
Writing about the Millbury Branch, 1995*

The Boston & Worcester opened its three-mile branch from Millbury Junction, near North Grafton, to Millbury in November 1837, the first of the B&W's six branches to be built. Its purpose was to access the highly successful textile mills in Millbury on the Blackstone River. Nine years earlier, in 1828, the Blackstone Canal opened between Providence & Worcester. It was not profitable and was sold to the Providence & Worcester Railroad. The P&W constructed some of its route adjacent to the canal right-of-way, opening in 1847, confronting the Boston & Albany with stiff north-south rail competition just a decade after the B&A built its branch.

The Boston & Worcester's 1850 Annual Report listed construction costs of $43,269, working expenses of $2,300, and income of only $1,250 for the branch. Yet management remained sanguine about its prospects: "The Millbury Branch brought about $10,000 of business to the main road, beside its proportion stated in the table. Although this business would have come in a great degree to this road at the period when it was built, the construction of other roads, recently, has afforded such other facilities that it is doubtful whether a large part of this business would not be lost, if the branch were to be discontinued."

Passenger service in 1893 comprised six daily Boston-Millbury round-trips and four Worcester-Millbury. In 1899 the nine scheduled passenger round-trips were shuttles to the mainline, and two of these were "mixed." Competing with the B&A in the 1890s was the Worcester

& Millbury, an electric railway absorbed into the Worcester & Suburban in 1895, and into the Worcester Consolidated in 1901. Such trolley systems had a sobering effect on railroad passenger revenues all over America. Thus by November 1919 the B&A ran only two and a half round-trips between Boston-Millbury and Worcester-Millbury. By April 1927 there was just a single Boston round-trip and a late afternoon train to Worcester (but no return). The February 1931 schedule had only the Boston round-trip, and this too was gone by late 1932.

The New Haven Railroad also had a depot in Millbury—though the two railroads were not physically connected—and offered daily except Sunday service on its Providence-Worcester line. For a time in the 1950s this train was covered by the unusual FCD Mack Railbus (one of two placed in service), named for its catalyst, Frederic C. Dumaine, Sr. The New England Transportation Company—a bus operation owned by the New Haven—provided Millbury with long distance (but not local) service to Fitchburg and Providence, as indicated in its September 1931 timetable, still offered in 1942.

By the 1970s, service on the Millbury branch was down to one weekly train. Conrail did not include the Millbury Branch when it took over operations from Penn Central in 1976. The rails were lifted in 1980, while most of the right-of-way was sold to the state for preservation.

Left: Penn Central SW-1500 No. 9530, built 1972, crosses Dorothy Pond in Millbury on its way to the main line in early 1974. Today's consist includes two box cars and caboose No. 18151 in the standard Penn Central jade green paint scheme. **Below:** *In October 1973 the local has arrived at Millbury Junction where the brakeman has thrown the switch to get us onto the main line. Two photos by William G. Dulmaine, Jr.*

Above: The Millbury local is "on the ground" at the Massachusetts Turnpike bridge in 1970. A Penn Central employee is assisting in the rerailing. William G. Dulmaine, Jr. photo.

Right: The crew of this shuttle train, with its baggage-coach combine, has taken a moment to pose for the photographer at Millbury Depot c. 1900. William G. Dulmaine, Jr. collection.

Over the Hill to Worcester 127

CARRYING THE MAIL

BRIAN R. SCACE, 1994

One and three quarters outside parcels equal one sack, except one box of baby chicks equals one sack and should be reported in the "Pouches and Sacks" column of train baggageman's report, Form M.D. 76.

B&A EMPLOYEES TIME-TABLE NO. 154 (April 25, 1948)

Mail trains are actually more complex than they might at first appear. The equipment offers some help in understanding the purposes of the varied consists, as do the consists themselves.

Though it is common practice to refer to the "mail and express" or "head-end" trains or equipment, a railroad's handling of U. S. Mail was a separate activity from that of an express company's business. The mail came under government contract and was subject to all the rules and regulations of the U. S. Postal Service. A Railway Post Office (RPO) was required to perform the same services as a fixed location post office, including stamp sales, accepting mail into the system, and protecting the mail in transit. Sorters were armed with .38 caliber Smith & Wessons. Although the rules for action required upon discovery of unlocked bags or other breaches of mail security were spelled out in the railroad company's employee timetable, the safety of the mail was the direct responsibility of the Postal Service. A train carrying a working RPO was not allowed to leave a station—schedules notwithstanding—until the handling of the mail was satisfactorily completed.

In contrast, express traffic was much like today's express or parcel shipments. Railroads handled express under contract to a private corporation such as Adams, American Express or, later, Railway Express Agency (REA). Although this traffic was as time dependent as mail, its security was the responsibility of the railroad by consignment, with no special mention in the employee timetable.

The equipment carrying U. S. Mail on the New York Central System was of two types: postal cars and mail storage cars. A typical working RPO consisted of a postal car, sometimes erroneously called an RPO itself, and one or more mail storage cars adjacent.

Mail is sorted en route in the postal car itself. It has a mail sorting area with the familiar "pigeon holes," mail bag catchers (or cranes) in the side doors for retrieving mail at speed, a small storage area for bags, and even a slot in the car side for people to post letters during station stops. This car was occupied by U. S. Postal employees only, though the car was railroad owned. The B&A owned its own postals of a modified USRA M1 pattern.

The postal car, having little storage room for bagged 1st class mail (let alone Parcel Post or 3rd class), usually was attached to a locked baggage car used as a mail storage car or "walk-through." It was normally unoccupied with all doors locked except the end door into the postal car. Standard baggage cars were used since end doors were required for postal employees to pass between cars while underway, both to retrieve mail for sorting or to store sorted bags. Intercity runs often included two "walk-through" cars, one on either end of the postal.

Standard baggage cars were also used as sealed mail storage cars, called "package" cars, with a single destination's mail locked inside. These were handled as pre-sorted lots and not opened until reaching their destination, such as a Boston-Chicago load. Or they were part of a working RPO in a subsequent train, such as a Boston to West Coast car handled as a locked car to Chicago then sorted as a "walk-through" west of Chicago.

Railroad employees or passengers were forbidden access to any cars in the RPO, except the conductor—when he had cause. On a solid mail train the railroad provided a "rider" car for employee use. On the B&A this was typically a coach or combine, although the NYC did build some specialized rider cars similar in dimension to express refrigerator cars, and these occasionally appeared on the B&A. Postal employees could ride these cars by showing "transportation," usually their post office ID with photo. On a passenger train with a working RPO the same regulations applied with the revenue space separated by lock from the RPO, similar to the rider car on a mail train.

On both the B&A and NYC, mail was handled in several different ways. Local mail was handled by an RPO for the stops between Boston and Albany as part of a daily "dog" local. The employee timetable provided that if an RPO were not attached to its regular run, the train on which it did run would assume the rights and scheduled stops of the RPO. This RPO would minimally be comprised of just a postal car, with perhaps an added "walk-through" if a large load was anticipated. Such locals sorted mail into bag lots for all stops. Any mail picked up locally to go beyond Boston or Albany was transferred to other RPOs at these cities. Some photos of local working RPOs show a baggage car in the head-end, working REA shipments. Such a car was not part of the RPO. Indeed, at stations, REA was handled on separately marked baggage wagons.

Next was the intercity "Working RPO" in a mail and express train, usually handling mail to another major city or another railroad. On the B&A this train carried mail to Boston from the west, much of it sorted by other RPOs on the NYC and locked in package cars turned over at Albany. Trains leaving Boston consisted of locked mail storage cars of sorted mail to zones west or whole car lots to individual cities. These had one or two postal cars with "walk-through" or open storage cars doing sorts from major pickups such as Worcester, Springfield, and Pittsfield—possibly done "on the fly"—and cleaning up the Boston sort. Then followed a host of sealed storage cars with mail to be sorted off-line or delivered in car lots, REA shipments in sealed cars separate from the RPO, and a rider car (or cars) with revenue passenger space.

Last was a "non-working" mail and express train, consisting of sealed mail cars with no working RPO, and not considered to be an RPO, since it performed no services required of a post office. These handled bulk 3rd class and Parcel Post, but not 1st class. The Boston Terminal Company employee timetable carried one of these as the Sunday-only "Paper Train" delivering Boston newspapers in bulk to points west.

Left: *The RPO was an American institution for the better part of a century. B&A Hudson No. 612 departs Millerton, New York, with local-express Train No. 14 for New York in August 1949. The station agent is taking the mail cart back to the depot after the pick up. John M. Wallace photo.*

Below: *This RPO cancellation was made on a postcard on Tuesday, June 16, 1906. RWJ collection.*

Assuming that magazines and individual out-of-state paper subscriptions were also handled, such 3rd class mail would be part of the Paper Train's consist, along with whatever other bulk REA and Parcel Post was made ready to move prior to midnight Saturday. Both types of intercity mail train were characterized as through traffic with minimal stops and maximum rights, by virtue of the timetable.

Such was the typical operation through the 20th Century steam era. Between the late 1940s and early 1960s several other types of equipment were found on these trains: displaced can-type milk cars in "packaged" or sealed mail storage service; converted troop sleepers; and "Flexi-Van" Container-On-Flat-Car (COFC) equipment. All were useful in mail storage service as "package" cars but, because of the absence of end doors, much of this stock was ill-suited to "walk-through" or open mail storage service. Thus did the old 60 ft. 6 in. baggage cars outlive these newcomers until the final withdrawal of U. S. Mail contracts in the late 1960s. Many marginal passenger trains then became money losers and were soon consigned to history books just as fast as the ICC consented.

Interestingly, storage cars in both mail and express service were freely interchanged with other roads, much like freight equipment, subject to ICC interchange regulations. Rarely were postal cars interchanged—except in the late 1960s when they were converted to storage cars. The B&A commonly hosted a fascinating mix of storage cars from other roads in the RPO and REA eras, always a colorful sight at South Station.

According to *The Railway Library, 1910*—a railroad advocate publication edited by one Slason Thompson—considerable propaganda was being disseminated to the effect that railroads were living high on the hog and should be paid less for such things as railway mail. According to Thompson, U. S. railroads were paid nearly $50 million in 1909 to carry the mail. For these fees, the railroads provided facilities at junctions and terminals, free delivery to post offices located within a quarter mile, and some 600 annual passes for postal officials. Where the U. S. collected 12.88¢ per pound of mail carried, it paid railroads 3¢ per pound to carry it, about 23¢ on the dollar.

The rate was determined by weighing a car's mail each day for 105 consecutive days once every four years, and determining the average for each route served. The railroads contended that not weighing every year deprived them of revenue from annual growth, which had risen consistently upward about 80% in ten years. They were further mightily annoyed that, as volume increased, rates went down.

The railroads thought they should be paid fares for carrying mail clerks, since they were furnished heat, water, toilets, and caused the same liability as a passenger in case of accident.

They complained that postal cars were useless for other carriage, and inefficient as well, carrying an eighth of what a baggage car would carry. In comparison to the 23% of revenue paid by the U. S. to railroads for mail, *The Railway Library, 1910* asserts that express companies paid 50 to 55% of gross receipts to the railroads. Reportedly revenue from express totaled $59,647,022 (2.47% of total earnings), while mail brought $49,380,783 (2.04% of total earnings); the profitability of express was attributed to the fact that it charged by distance whereas postal fees were standardized, causing the Post Office to operate at a loss. Much was made of express companies paying full value for all services at stations and aboard trains, and their assuming all liability for employees.

Thompson determined that there were 3.95 cars in the average U. S. passenger train, 11% of which were mail cars, and that an average passenger train earned $1.26 per train mile. Instead of paying 11% of earnings, mail cars paid 7.5%, about 2/3 of what they should be on equal footing. Contrast this notion with the situation after World War II, when myriad passenger lines held on only because of the mail contracts, and the railroads were mighty pleased to have the cash.

ONBOARD A RAILWAY POST OFFICE

FRANK X. LUNDY, 1995

We had to catch the mail on the road. I'm sure you've seen pictures of that operation. When we had the steam engines, most of the guys would wear handkerchiefs around their necks and you'd make sure you had your goggles on. You got a cinder in your eye and if you weren't wearing your goggles, you went to the hospital and didn't get anything if you were off the job. You'd face your back to the direction of the train and pull the catcher down. It had a handle on it and you'd catch the mail and pull it in. You'd have to look out every now and then to see your reference points. There might be a certain barn and you'd know it was only about thirty seconds from there. Every now and then the guys would catch the side of a freight car or something like that. They were mostly wooden then and you'd pull in a little lumber. If you missed a catch you'd make out a report. You'd say it was snowing, even in the middle of August, or raining so hard you couldn't see, or the sun was in your eyes, at night no less!

Frank X. Lundy
THE RAILROADERS (1983)

I started on the B&A between Christmas and New Year's in 1938. I got up to Boston and at South Station there was some kind of big to-do going on—all the kids had beanies on—there was a big commotion. A policeman told me it was Vic Damone arriving for a big show. He was just 18 or 19 then, and already a star.

I lived in Tarrytown, New York then, and would travel up to Albany—the conductor would often let me sleep in a deadhead Pullman for a couple of hours—to start my run. The work cycle was 14 days, with six on and eight off. The formula was that for every six hours, 25 minutes you worked on the railroad, that was worth eight hours in the post office. Every other Saturday I'd get off at Springfield and go home on the New Haven. It was faster that way, and one of my buddies would cover for me to Albany.

The layover in Boston was nine or ten hours, and I could get a cot and a blanket at the railroad YMCA for 35¢. There was a big saloon right across from South Station where we often ate; sometimes we went up to Scollay Square. My layover in Tarrytown was longer, thankfully, about 26 hours. My two winters on the B&A were very cold. I remember the burning pitch torches they used to keep the switches from freezing. On really cold days, sometimes the heat wouldn't get back to all the cars on the long trains, and then you'd hear the complaining!

Downhill to Westfield we made little local stops where the people were very proud of their local temperatures—it was always 2° colder than anywhere else. They were all lying but it was fun hearing them carry on.

I worked the express trains that handled mail in the big places: Chatham, Pittsfield, Springfield, Palmer, Worcester, and Framingham. Mostly the local trains handled the smaller towns. There was a nice postmistress in western Massachusetts I remember. One Christmas time she baked a birthday cake for Eldon Ryan, one of our mail clerks from Amesbury, Massachusetts, the northeastern-most town in the state. The post office people were always thoughtful like that.

Since most of the B&A run was in Massachusetts, it was mostly men from the state covering these trains. I started

Above: An RPO cancellation made Thursday, May 20, 1909 at the Albany, New York terminal. RWJ collection.

Left: A NYC L-3a Mohawk has a westbound B&A mail and passenger train with a working RPO at Palmer on a cold, gray March day in 1949. John M. Wallace photo.

with the Post Office in 1936. To get in, you took a test and had to get a 95% score to be hired. I think 180,000 people took that test. It was the Depression and nobody had work. When the War came I joined a construction battalion in the Navy Seabees, and was able to put my civil engineering training to good use. My proudest achievement was making working drawings of the *U. S. S. United States*, and having them take all my stuff and publish it in a brochure.

After the War, I transferred into the Railway Mail Service, where I was able to take all my seniority with me, plus the two extra grades I'd earned in the Navy. Then I was two grades over everybody in the mail cars—I got a big kick out of that.

We worked for the Post Office, of course, not the railroad. Our Chief Clerk was a Mr. O'Hare who worked out of Boston. His boss was the Second Assistant Postmaster General in Washington, rather than the local post office.

It was wonderful working on those railway mail cars, you were never lonely. You had eight mail clerks—at least—working at a time, with a Clerk-in-Charge as head man. Every one of those guys came up from the ranks, all Civil Service, and they were all good guys. Everybody got along. You had to, working close like that.

Top: Working in a cramped Railway Post Office could be a challenge. You were constantly on your feet in the swaying, lurching car, and you shared the space with perhaps seven colleagues. This Boston & Albany RPO is a turn-of-the-century wooden car. Photo courtesy of the Society for the Preservation of New England Antiquities.

Above: B&A mail train No. 148 with a working RPO was photographed behind E-8 No. 4065 circa 1962, probably near Riverside, judging from the recently vacated wide ballast. Leon Onofri collection.

132 Boston & Albany

Left: *The eastbound* New England States *has departed Worcester Union Station behind an E-8A, an E-7B, and an E-7A, and is heading through the yard on Wednesday, August 2, 1967. Compare this sunny scene with that on the next page.*

Right: *E-8A No. 4053, E-7B No. 4107, and another E-8 head the* New England States *at Worcester on Saturday, December 16, 1961. This handsome "Century" green was applied to just three passenger diesels—these two plus E-8 No. 4083—and then only for a short time. Two photos by John F. Kane.*

Below left: *A railroad strike in 1946 was the cause of these four 0-8-0 steam switchers standing cold and idle at the Worcester round house. Identifiable are Nos. 30 and 36 (Class U-33), and No. 65 (Class U-2l). Stanley H. Smith photo/E. James Gibbons collection.*

Below: *NYC No. 6916, an 0-6-0 switcher, is taking on water at the Worcester round house c. 1946. Indeed it appears she is overflowing at the moment the camera was triggered. Stanley H. Smith photo/Norton D. Clark collection.*

Over the Hill to Worcester 133

During a 1947 blizzard, Stanley H. Smith battled icy weather in Worcester to record the railroad working through the storm. **Above:** A switcher toils away in the B&A yard amidst heavily falling snow. The tower of the former Union Station is visible in the distance at right. **Below:** NYC L-4b Mohawk No. 3131 heads up the the Paul Revere, carrying sleeping cars eastbound from Chicago, Cincinnati, Cleveland, Detroit, and St. Louis to Boston. The fireman braves the elements atop the tender as water is taken on. **Right:** A powerful B&A Class A-1c Berkshire pushes up the snow westbound past Union Station. Note eastbound train at center right, express car at far right, and sleeper at far left. Three photos from the E. James Gibbons collection.

In Volume II: Worcester to Albany

From the riverbed near Woronoco, Thomas J. McNamara photographed the westbound Knickerbocker *in October 1950, in this vibrant autumn setting. A NYC Mohawk is at the head of a colorfully mixed consist of both old and new B&A and NYC coaches, Pullmans, and a diner.*

Covering Steam • Diesel • Boston & Albany • New York Central • Penn Central • Amtrak • Conrail

V. To Springfield and the Connecticut River

Worcester Union Station • "Working B&A's Freight" by Robert Roche • Webster Branch
Spencer Branch • North Brookfield Branch • "On the Extra Board in Wartime" by Andy Payne
"On the Extra Board in Peacetime" by Robert Gardner
Ware River Branch • "Ware River Observer" by Donald S. Robinson
"Ware River Crossing Tender" by Reverend Walter H. Smith • Athol Branch

VI. Over the Mountain

"In the Tower" by D. Robert McCulloch • Selkirk Branch • Signals on the B&A • Post Road
North Adams Branch • "Riding Up to North Adams" by Clarence Gardner • Hudson Branch
"Riding the Mountain" by Brian R. Scace

VII. Railroad Life in the Berkshires

"Pittsfield Yard Master" by William Gregor Ryan • "Telegraph Interlude" by Mac Sebree
"An Agent at Work" by Frank E. Leonard
"Nellie MacDonald and the Hinsdale Depot" by Robert Willoughby Jones

VIII: Magnificent Stations: The Legacy of Henry Hobson Richardson

Epilogue by Brian Solomon • Bibliography • Index